RANGER RICK
NATIONAL WILDLIFE FEDERATION

Kids' Guide to
FISHING

THE YOUNG ANGLER'S GUIDE TO CATCHING MORE AND BIGGER FISH

To use the compass in this book, hold it flat, using both hands. Turn your body until the red North arrow is pointing straight ahead. That's your North!

By Dave Maas

Walter Foster Jr.

Brimming with creative inspiration, how-to projects, and useful information to enrich your everyday life, Quarto Knows is a favorite destination for those pursuing their interests and passions. Visit our site and dig deeper with our books into your area of interest: Quarto Creates, Quarto Cooks, Quarto Homes, Quarto Lives, Quarto Drives, Quarto Explores, Quarto Gifts, or Quarto Kids.

Written by Dave Maas

The National Wildlife Federation & Ranger Rick contributors: Children's Publication Staff, Licensing Staff and in-house naturalist David Mizejewski.

© National Wildlife Federation. All rights reserved.
www.RangerRick.com
First Published in 2017 by Walter Foster Publishing, an imprint of The Quarto Group.
6 Orchard Road, Suite 100, Lake Forest, CA 92630, USA.
T (949) 380-7510 F (949) 380-7575 www.QuartoKnows.com

Walter Foster Jr. titles are also available at discount for retail, wholesale, promotional, and bulk purchase. For details, contact the Special Sales Manager by email at specialsales@quarto.com or by mail at The Quarto Group, Attn: Special Sales Manager, 401 Second Avenue North, Suite 310, Minneapolis, MN 55401 USA.

ISBN: 978-1-63322-382-0

Printed in China
10 9 8 7 6 5 4 3 2

TABLE OF CONTENTS

What Can I Catch?... 4

What Tackle Do I Need?.. 22

How Do I Make a Fish Bite?.............................. 48

Is It a Keeper?.. 76

A MESSAGE FROM

If you're like most young anglers, you don't care what kind of fish you catch as long as you get something. After all, while it's fun just to be outside spending time away from home (chores) and school (tests), fishing is the most fun when you catch fish!

By reading this book, you'll learn great tips for catching more sunfish, bass, carp, catfish, and all sorts of other freshwater fish. This book is also filled with little-known fish facts, like: Did you know that some fish you catch are older than you are? It's true!

It won't take you a lot of time to read this book. That's good because you'll have more hours for fishing! But bring this book along on your next fishing trip, and use this compass to help you find your way. Somewhere in these pages is the one thing that will make all the difference between getting skunked and catching the biggest fish of your life!

Happy fishing!

Ranger Rick

WHAT CAN I
CATCH?

No matter where you live, you'll find **great fishing** for some type of fish. It may be catfish or sunfish in a local farm pond, carp in a nearby river, or crappies and bass in the lake across town.

The beginning of this book shows you where different fish types (called **species**) live. As you page through this chapter, check out the **small, colored maps** to see which species live in your state. And look closely at the drawings of the fish so you can tell what you have landed.

So what **species** do you think will be your favorite to catch?

SUNFISH

Sunfish are a family of 37 different species of fish, including crappies, bluegills, pumpkinseeds, and spotted sunfish. Spotted sunfish are small fish that usually measure 3 to 9 inches long from the nose to the tip of the tail. They can weigh up to a pound or more, but are often much smaller. Spotted sunfish are fun to catch because they fight very hard for their size.

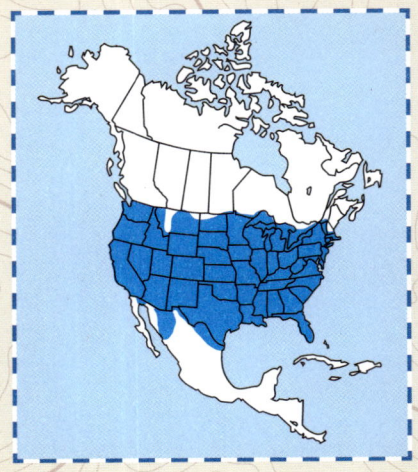

SPOTTED SUNFISH

SLIME Just as a coat protects people from harsh weather, slime protects a fish from diseases.

FINS Always moving, fins let the fish move in any direction it wants to go, even backward!

Spotted sunfish are short and skinny, so they can easily move around in the weeds to find food. Their shape also allows them to quickly hide in weeds and not get eaten by bigger fish.

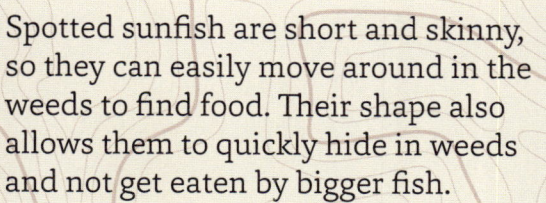

GILLS Sunfish use their gills to breathe under water.

EYES Sunfish have eyes on the sides of their head so they can see food and bigger fish all around them.

MOUTH Spotted sunfish have a small mouth for eating little things, usually stuff about the size of a pea.

CRAPPIES

Crappies are part of the sunfish family. There are two types: the white crappie and the black crappie. Most of the crappies people catch measure from 5 to 12 inches long.

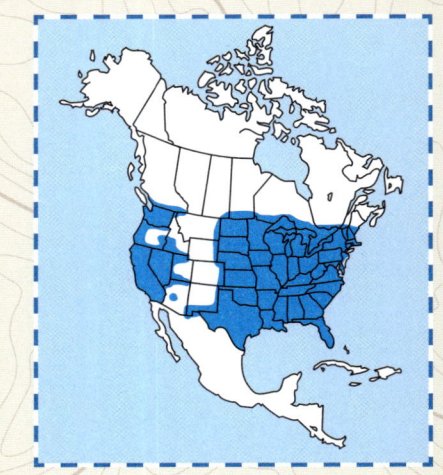

BLACK CRAPPIE

FINS A black crappie's larger fins have scattered black specks.

SHAPE Crappies have a bullet-shaped front, which helps them swim very fast to catch speedy minnows.

8

Crappies have lots of nicknames, but the most popular one is probably "papermouth." Fishermen call them this because of the paper-thin skin surrounding the fish's lips. In fact, lots of crappies are lost during the fight because anglers pull too hard and tear the hook from the fish's mouth.

papermouth

EYES Crappies can see very well after dark. They often begin eating just after sunset—a time when smart anglers are still fishing.

MOUTH A crappie has a large mouth, which allows it to eat minnows and big insects.

BASS

There are many kinds of bass. The ones you are most likely to catch are rock bass, largemouth bass, and smallmouth bass. In some parts of the country, you can catch all three kinds in the same lake.

Rock bass are easy to catch. They'll bite almost anything, and you can often catch the same fish over and over again.

Largemouth bass and smallmouth bass are more difficult to catch—but not impossible. Many times these bass bury themselves in thick weeds or make awesome jumps to throw the hook.

ROCK BASS

SIDES Rock bass can change color from light brown to green to blend in with their surroundings.

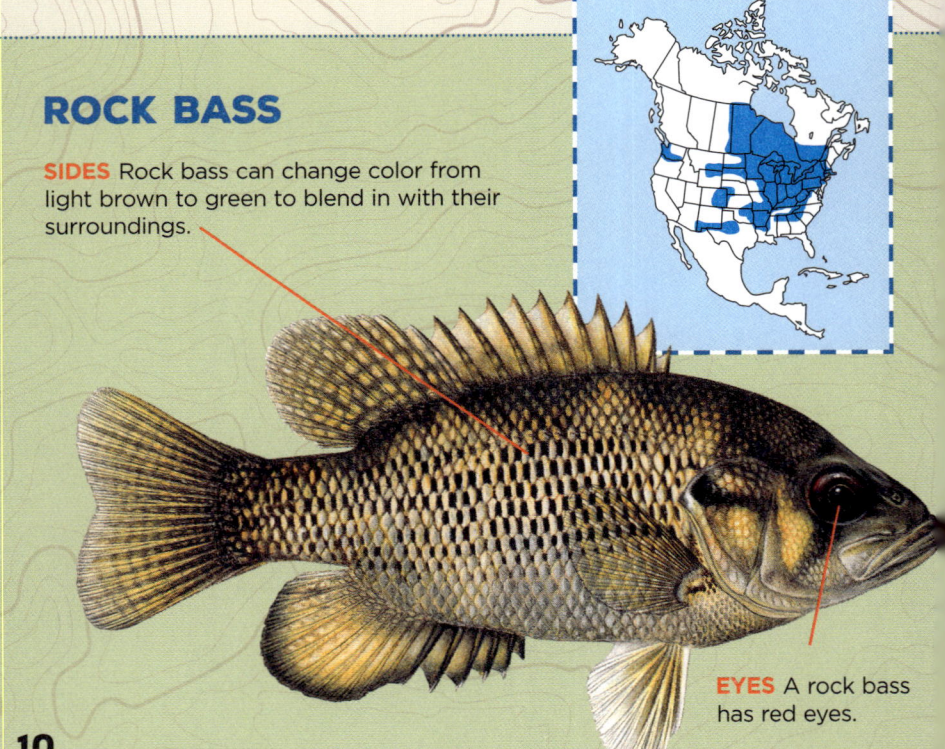

EYES A rock bass has red eyes.

LARGEMOUTH BASS

SIDES Largemouths have light green sides with a black stripe from the gills to the tail.

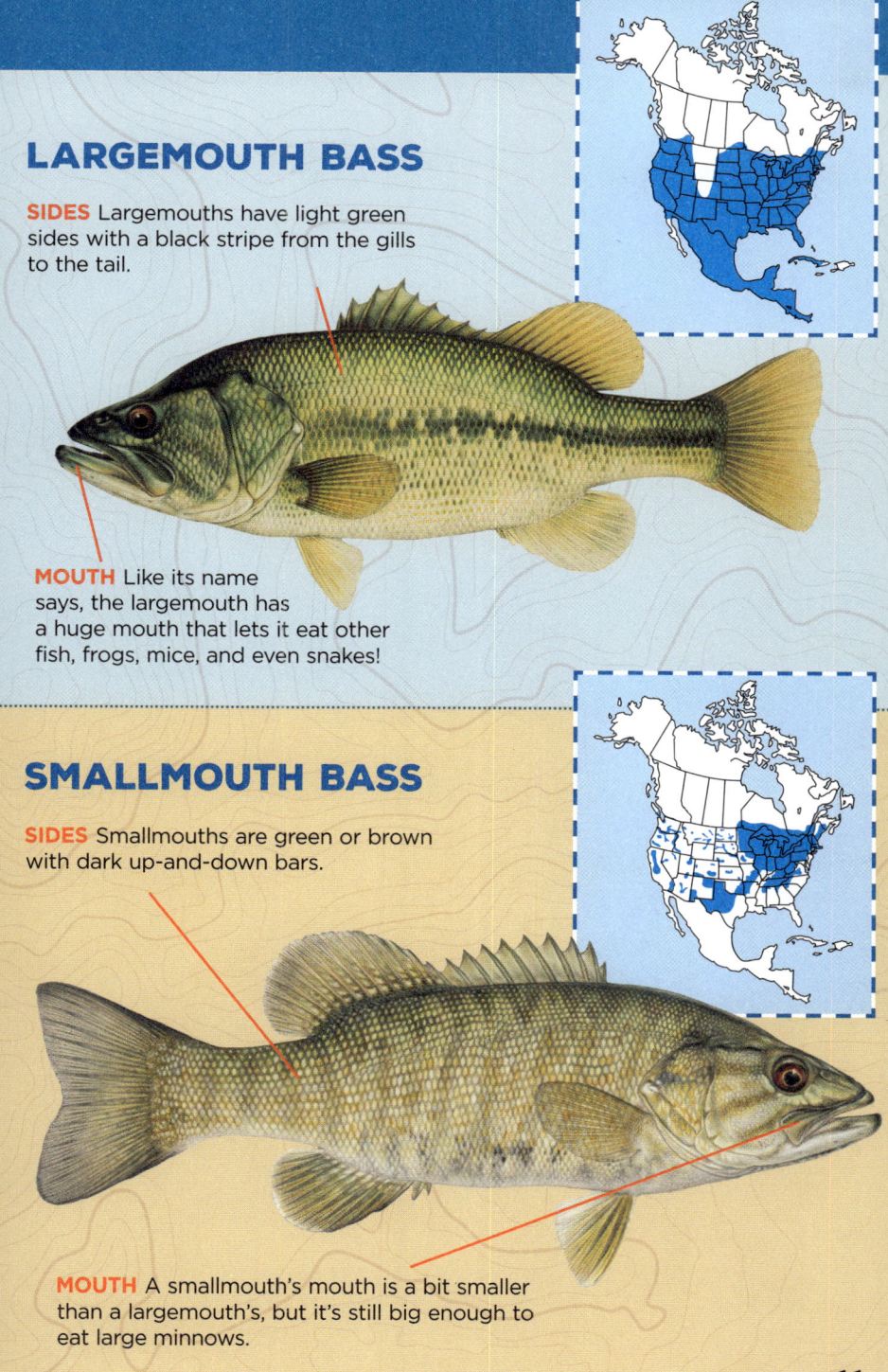

MOUTH Like its name says, the largemouth has a huge mouth that lets it eat other fish, frogs, mice, and even snakes!

SMALLMOUTH BASS

SIDES Smallmouths are green or brown with dark up-and-down bars.

MOUTH A smallmouth's mouth is a bit smaller than a largemouth's, but it's still big enough to eat large minnows.

11

CARP

Carp were introduced to North America more than 100 years ago. Now, carp have adapted so well and reproduced so quickly that they are considered to be a nuisance fish. Some carp, like the Asian carp, can cause damage to the ecosystem and compete with other fish for food and space.

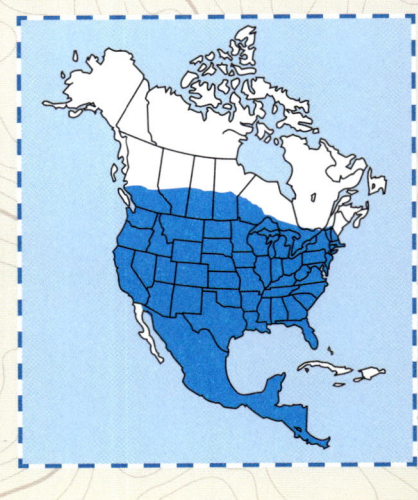

COMMON CARP

TAIL Carp use their powerful tail to put up a good fight when hooked.

Carp living in streams and small rivers usually weigh 1 to 5 pounds, but carp in big rivers and lakes grow to huge sizes, sometimes more than 40 pounds! Catching a big carp can be a real challenge, especially because they scare easily.

SIDES A big carp has thick scales larger than a quarter. Carp are usually yellow or golden brown.

MOUTH Carp have small whiskers, or **barbels**, on both sides of the upper jaw.

CATFISH

Catfish are a family of 51 different species, including bullhead catfish. Catfish and bullheads are easy to identify because of their long whiskers. Bullheads don't get very big and they have a rounded tail. Catfish have forked tails and they can get huge— the biggest catfish ever caught weighed more than 120 pounds.

CATFISH

SIDES Depending on the type of catfish, the sides are green, brown, or bluish silver.

Channel catfish range

MOUTH Catfish have long whiskers called **barbels** that sense taste and texture, helping catfish find food.

It's fun to fish for catfish and bullheads because they eat just about anything. Some of the best baits are the ones that stink the worst! You can try using worms, live or dead minnows, dried chicken blood, or homemade dough balls.

BULLHEADS

SIDES Depending on the type of bullhead, the sides are yellow, brown, green, or gold.

Black bullhead range

MOUTH The longest barbels are usually dark brown to black.

NORTHERN PIKE & MUSKIES

Both the northern pike and the muskie are built for one thing—speed. Their long, sleek bodies are perfect for swimming fast and chasing down prey. These fish have huge mouths and often attack and eat fish almost half their own length. In other words, a 1-foot-long pike or muskie will think nothing of eating a 6-inch-long minnow!

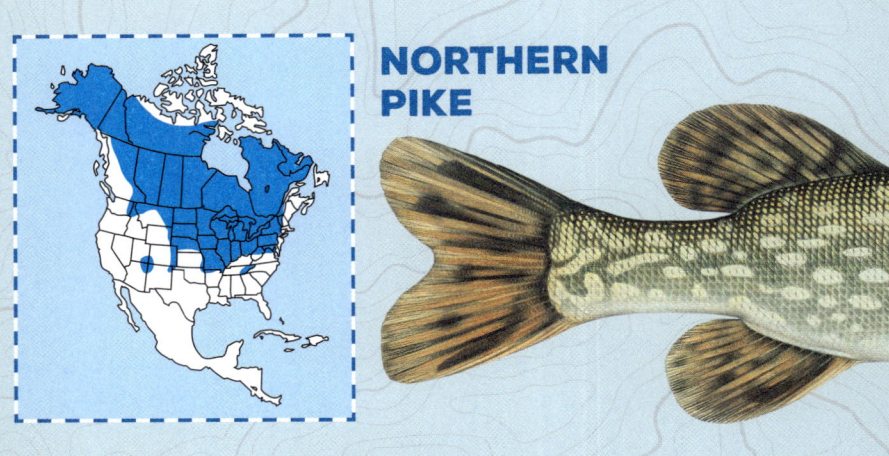

NORTHERN PIKE

MUSKIE

TAIL The tips of a muskie's tail are more pointed than those of a northern pike.

Northern pike are also called jackfish or gators. Small northerns (1 to 3 pounds) are often called "snakes" and "hammer handles."

Teeth on a northern pike

The biggest muskie ever caught measured almost 5 feet long. Northern pike don't grow as big, but they can still reach 4 feet in length.

SIDES Pike have dark green sides with rows of light spots.

MOUTH Large teeth help the northern pike (and muskie) hold small fish before they're swallowed headfirst.

SIDES The muskie has dark bars or spots on a light green background.

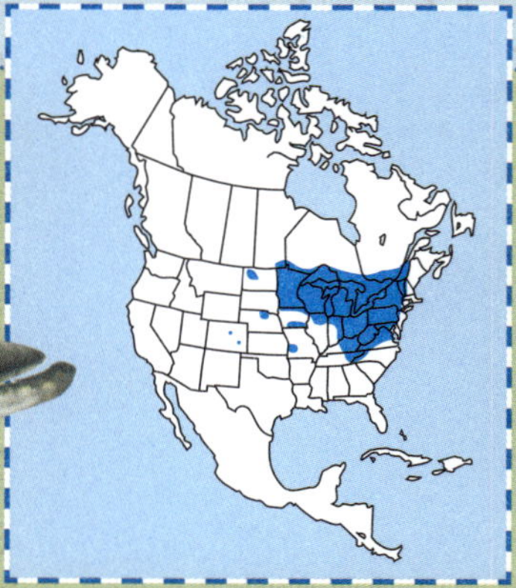

PERCH & WALLEYES

If you've ever eaten fresh perch or walleyes, you know how great they taste. These species don't fight as hard as bass and northern pike, but lots of people like to fish for them because they make such a great meal.

PERCH

SIDES Perch have yellow sides with six to nine dark bars.

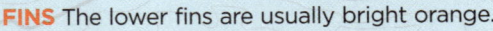

FINS The lower fins are usually bright orange.

Like sunfish and rock bass, perch are easy to catch. Walleyes are much harder to catch.

Perch usually measure 4 to 10 inches in length. Walleyes get much bigger, sometimes measuring more than 2½ feet long and weighing more than 10 pounds.

WALLEYES

SIDES The sides are olive green with gold flecks.

TAIL The tip on the bottom of a walleye's tail is white.

EYES Walleyes can see better at night than most other fish.

TROUT & SALMON

Many types of trout and salmon are found in North America. The most popular trout species is the rainbow trout. If you've ever hooked one, you know that few other fish fight as hard or jump as high from the water. Most rainbows measure 8 to 20 inches long.

RAINBOW TROUT

FINS Small black spots cover the rainbow's dorsal fin and tail.

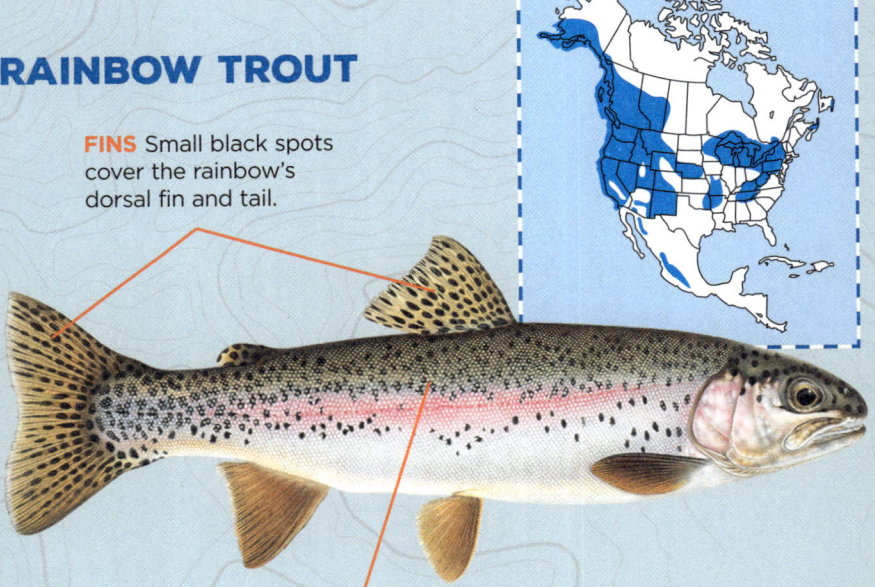

SIDES A rainbow has a pink stripe and lots of black spots on its side.

Of all the salmon species, the Chinook grows the biggest, often weighing 30 to 40 pounds. These fish are so strong that they sometimes pull all the line off a fisherman's reel before escaping!

Chinook salmon

Chinook salmon are often called king salmon. Coho salmon are called silvers, and sockeye salmon are known as red salmon.

CHINOOK SALMON

SIDES Chinook salmon have silver sides with black spots on their back and tail.

TAIL The powerful tail helps salmon jump up river rapids and small waterfalls.

WHAT TACKLE DO I NEED?

As with any other sport, having the **right equipment** for fishing is very important. But you don't have to spend a lot of money buying every high-tech, flashy lure you see hanging on the wall of your local tackle shop.

This chapter will show you all the **best lures and live baits** for the species you want to catch. You'll also see the best rods, reels, lines, and knots.

This chapter also has great photos to teach you how to cast for both **accuracy and distance**. Many times the difference between catching a fish and not catching a fish is being able to make a good long cast to the right spot. After reading this chapter and practicing a bit, you'll be casting like a pro.

SAFETY FIRST

To have fun while fishing, you first have to be safe. Below are some important rules to remember whenever you're fishing.

Everyone (adults included!) should wear a life jacket when on the water. Young anglers (under 14 or so) or anyone fishing alone should especially wear a life jacket at all times. Why? Because even if you are a good swimmer, you could hit your head and get knocked out during a fall from the boat into the water. If you're knocked out and not wearing a life jacket, you will drown if no one is there to pull you to safety.

Never wade into the water unless you're supervised by an adult. A deep drop-off might be close to shore, and you could end up in water that's over your head.

Take along a few bandages in your tackle box. It's easy to get small cuts when handling hooks and taking off fish. A bandage will keep the cut clean.

Make sure no one is behind you before making a cast. Remember, those hooks are sharp! See pages 46 and 47 for the correct way to cast.

Never grab a fish near where it's hooked. The fish might wiggle and you could get a hook in your hand. See pages 78–81 for tips on safely handling fish.

If you do get a hook in you, stay calm and get help from an adult. It's best to let a doctor remove the hook.

It's a good idea to wear a baseball hat and polarized sunglasses. These items not only protect your eyes and head from other angler's hooks, but they also help you see into the water to spot fish.

Carry sunblock and bug spray in your tackle box, and use them when needed. The more comfortable you are, the longer you will be able to fish.

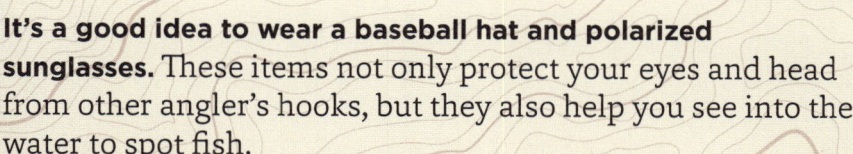

FOR PARENTS

If you are not totally comfortable in and around water, by all means insist that everyone in the boat wear a life jacket at all times. "Better safe than sorry" is the best advice when it comes to boating.

HOOKS, LINES, SINKERS & BOBBERS

HOOKS

A mistake lots of young anglers make when getting ready to fish is using the wrong size hook for the species they want to catch. Usually these kids tie on a hook that's too big, and it won't go into the fish's mouth. Picture trying to shove a whole pizza into your mouth at one time, and you'll get the idea!

Let's say you want to catch sunfish. Remember, sunfish eat foods like tiny bugs and small worms. Your hook needs to be just big enough to hold your choice of live bait, but not so big that the sunnie can't easily eat it.

Crappies have slightly bigger mouths than sunfish, so you should use a little bit bigger hook to catch crappies.

crappie hook

sunfish hook

Hooks come in all shapes and sizes. For most of your fishing, you'll need hooks from size 1/0 (big) to 12 (very small). The chart below shows the actual size of these hooks. The chart on page 28 gives you tips on what size hook to use for different fish.

HOOKS SHOWN ACTUAL SIZE

1/0

1

2

4

6

8

10

12

TO CATCH THIS CRAPPIE, your hook should be about size 6. For smaller sunfish, use a size 10.

This chart shows the best hook size to use for different fish species. As a rule, whenever you can't decide between two hook sizes, choose the smaller one—you'll catch more fish!

HOOK CHART

SPECIES	HOOK SIZE
sunfish	10
perch	8
crappies	6
trout	6
rock bass	4
bullheads	2
walleyes	2
smallmouth bass	1
carp	1
catfish	1/0
largemouth bass	1/0
northern pike	1/0 or larger
muskies	1/0 or larger
salmon	1/0 or larger

DID YOU KNOW?

"Test" is the strength of the fishing line you use.

LINE

Having good fishing line is very important if you want to cast far and land the fish that take your bait. For all of your fishing, you should use monofilament line. This line comes in all sorts of colors, but your best bet is to use the clear stuff. Why? Because it's hard for the fish to see (so you'll get lots of strikes), but it's easy for you to see (for tying knots and getting out tangles).

What size line should you choose? That depends on the species you're after. Use the chart below the next time you buy fishing line.

SPECIES	LINE SIZE
sunfish	4-pound test
perch	4-pound test
crappies	4-pound test
trout	4-pound test
rock bass	4-pound test
bullheads	4-pound test
walleyes	6-pound test
smallmouth bass	6-pound test
carp	8-pound test
catfish	10-pound test or higher
largemouth bass	10-pound test or higher
northern pike	12-pound test or higher
muskies	20-pound test or higher
salmon	20-pound test or higher

LINE CHART

SINKERS

Like hooks, sinkers come in a million shapes and sizes. With all these choices, how are you supposed to know what to use? It's simple—get a variety of **split shot**. This is the type of sinker that you pinch onto the line. Some types of split shot are reusable, which means that you can pinch them open to take them off your line. Split shot can be used when fishing with a bobber or when fishing with live bait on the bottom (page 52).

A variety of split shot

Reusable split shot are pinched closed to stay on the line. You pinch them open to take them off the line. Try to find a plastic pack of split shot that contains several sizes. That way, you'll always have the size you need.

BOBBERS

When you fish for sunfish, crappies, or rock bass, you'll often need a bobber. A bobber keeps your bait at just the right spot. You've probably used a round, red-and-white plastic bobber before, and this type works OK. But there is a better choice, and it's just as easy to use.

The **spring-lock bobber** (below) attaches to your line with a single tiny spring on the bottom of the bobber. Because of its shape, this bobber is easy for a fish to pull under. You'll catch a lot more fish with this type of bobber than you will with the round bobber. It's also easier to cast because it cuts through the wind much like an arrow.

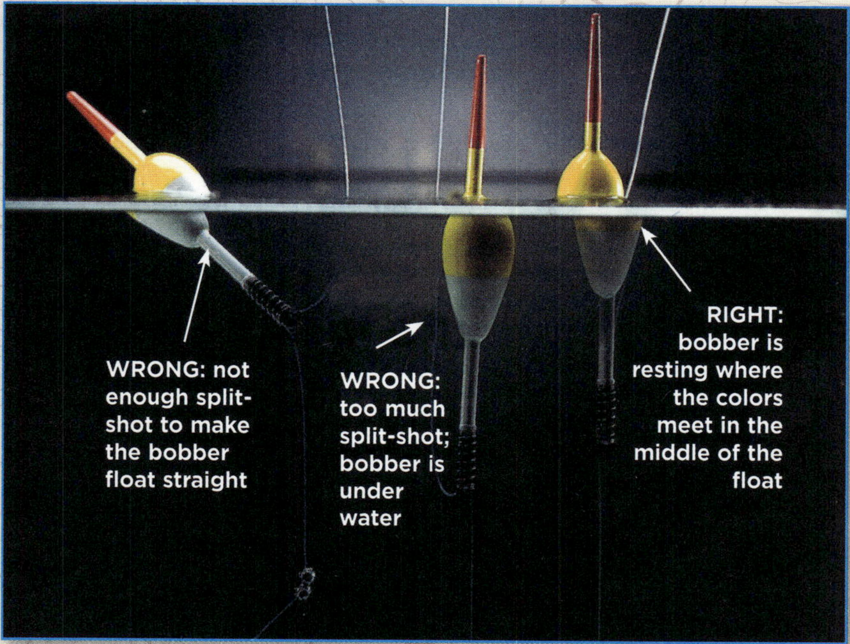

WRONG: not enough split-shot to make the bobber float straight

WRONG: too much split-shot; bobber is under water

RIGHT: bobber is resting where the colors meet in the middle of the float

You want to use just enough split shot on your line so that half of the spring-lock bobber sticks out of the water.

LURES & LIVE BAIT

Now it's time to get serious about stocking your tackle box with the lures a fish will strike. You'll learn about live bait later in this section.

LURES

Lots of kids think they need the latest "secret" lure to catch fish. Wrong! What they really need is the right lure for the right time and place. In other words, any lure in your box could be the secret lure if you know when and how to use it. These are some of the best lure types for catching different kinds of fish.

FEATHER JIG
sunfish, crappies, yellow perch, rock bass

BEETLE SPIN
sunfish, crappies, yellow perch, bass

TWISTER TAIL JIG
all species of fish

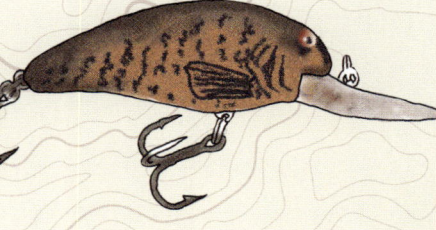

PLASTIC WORM
bass (especially largemouth)

SPINNERBAIT
northern pike, bass, muskie

CRANKBAIT
northern pike, bass, muskie, walleye, salmon, trout

TOPWATER LURE
northern pike, bass, muskie

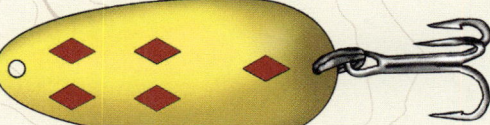

SPOON
northern pike, muskie, walleye, salmon, trout

Maybe the hardest decision to make before you start fishing is what size lure to use. It's actually pretty easy if you ask yourself the following question: **What size food does the fish I'm trying to catch usually eat?** For example, a sunfish usually eats bugs less than 1 inch long, so you should use a lure less than 1 inch long. It's that simple!

Lots of kids (and adults) use lures that are way too big for sunfish and crappies. Remember the kid trying to eat a whole pizza in one bite? It can't be done! The chart below shows you what size lures to use for different fish species.

What about lure type? Let's say you're standing on a fishing pier getting ready to fish for crappies. From the chart below, you've decided to use a 2-inch-long lure.

LURE SIZE CHART

SPECIES	LURE LENGTH IN INCHES
sunfish	½ to 1
perch	1 to 2
rock bass	1 to 2
crappies	1 to 2½
trout	1 to 3
walleyes	1 to 4
smallmouth	1 to 4
largemouth bass	3 to 6
northern pike	4 to 8
salmon	4 to 8
muskies	5 to 12

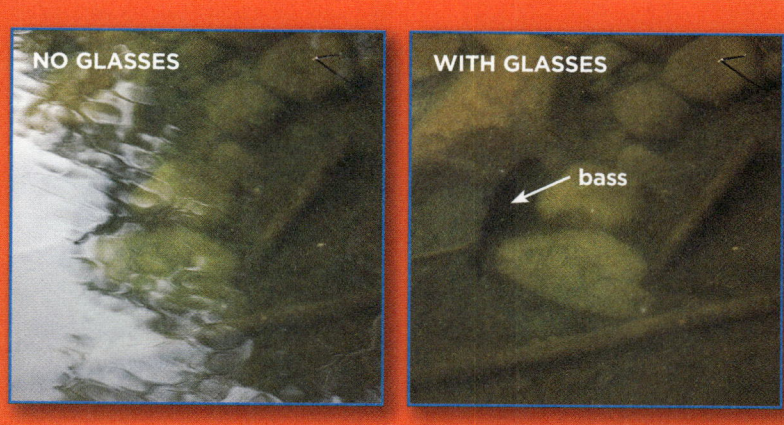

Polarized sunglasses are great for spotting fish and fish hiding spots. Without glasses it's hard to see into the water because of the glare. With polarized sunglasses it's easy to spot a big bass waiting to be caught!

But should you use a 2-inch jig or a 2-inch spinner?

Ask yourself this question: How deep are the crappies living? Now you probably won't know exactly, but you can make a good guess by looking into the water with your polarized sunglasses. Do you see lots of bug life and minnow life in the shallows? If so, the crappies will probably be shallow feeding on the bugs and minnows, and you should use a shallow-running lure like the spinner. If the water looks "dead," and you don't see any bug or minnow life, then the crappies are probably a bit deeper and you should use the jig. Get the idea?

Another great way to find out how deep the fish are located is to ask someone working at a tackle shop. These people have a good idea of fish location through the year because they talk to successful anglers every day.

LIVE BAIT

As with artificial lures, your choice of live bait depends on the kind of fish you want to catch. Check out the list below for the most popular types and sizes of live bait for each species.

Sunfish: tiny worms, grubs, leeches, grass shrimp, crickets, grasshoppers

Perch: small minnows, worms, leeches, crickets, grubs, crayfish tails

Crappies: small minnows, grubs

Trout: 2- to 3-inch minnows, worms, grasshoppers

Rock bass: will eat anything you can find

Bullheads: worms, leeches, crayfish, snails, crickets

Walleyes: nightcrawlers, leeches, 2- to 4-inch minnows

Smallmouth bass: crayfish, 2- to 4-inch minnows, nightcrawlers, hellgrammites

Carp: nightcrawlers

Catfish: nightcrawlers, crayfish, live or dead minnows (small minnows for small catfish; 6- to 12-inch minnows for big catfish)

Largemouth bass: 3- to 6-inch minnows, crayfish, nightcrawlers

Northern pike: 4- to 8-inch minnows

Muskies: 6- to 12-inch minnows

How you hook live bait is very important. It must stay on your hook during a cast and also look natural to the fish. The pictures on pages 51 and 53 show you the most popular methods for rigging live bait. Remember, use the correct hook size for the fish you're after (if you're not sure, turn back to the hook chart on p. 28).

MINNOW TIP

If you buy minnows from a bait shop, make sure to have the person behind the counter put them in an oxygen bag. This is the best way to keep your minnows alive and strong until you are ready to use them. Once you get to the lake, you can open the bag and put the minnows in a bucket.

HOW TO TIE A GOOD FISHING KNOT

After all the time and effort it takes to hook a big fish, the last thing you want is to lose it because your knot comes untied. Here's some good advice: **Use the knot shown on the next page,** and this won't happen to you. It may be a bit tricky at first, but after some practice, you'll be able to tie it in complete darkness. Give it a try!

KNOT TIPS

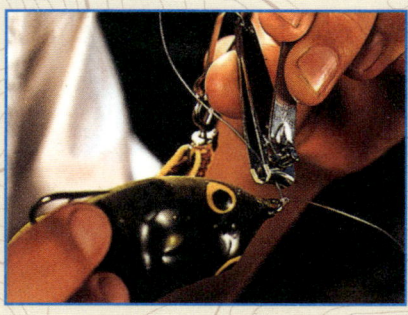

LEAVE A LITTLE EXTRA LINE when clipping the free end of your knot. Some knots slip a bit when a fish is pulling hard, and the extra line will keep the knot from coming loose.

WET THE KNOT before snugging it up. This helps tighten the knot without making it weaker.

1 Start by passing the line through the eye of the hook twice from the same side, leaving a double loop next to the eye.

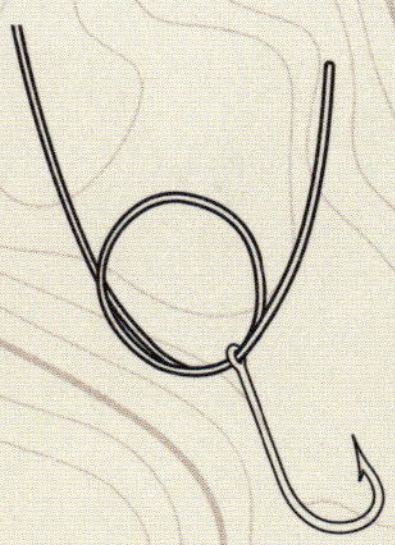

2 Wrap the free end about five times.

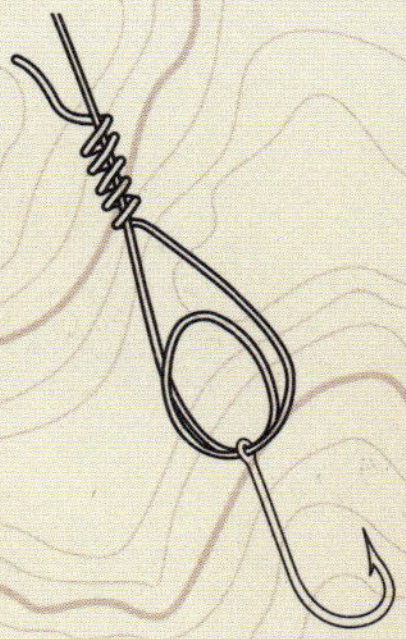

3 Push the free end through the double loop.

4 Wet the line, and tighten the knot. Cut the free end about 1/4 inch from the knot.

THE TRILENE KNOT

RODS, REELS & HOW TO CAST FARTHER THAN YOUR FRIENDS

Before the invention of high-tech fishing rods and reels, people used long cane poles, with a short section of fishing line tied to the end. Cane poles work great for fishing close to the boat or dock, but if you want to cast, you're out of luck.

The rods and reels you see in tackle shops allow you to cast a long way with ease. But you need to have the right kind of rod and reel for the type of fish you're after.

REELS

SPINCASTING REELS: Spincast reels are often called **push-buttons** or **closed-face reels.** These are the best reels to start fishing with because they hardly ever tangle, and they cast pretty far. The other great thing is that they don't cost a lot of money.

SPINNING REELS: These are the reels that have a bail that must be flipped to make a cast. They are also called **open-face reels.** They are harder to learn to use than a spincast reel and are more expensive. Spinning reels cast lures a bit farther than a spincast reel.

BAITCASTING REELS: With this type of reel, you must hold your thumb on the line spool during the cast to keep from getting a tangle. Baitcasters are the hardest type of reels to learn to use. Many adults never get good with these reels. When you get a tangle with a baitcasting reel, it's called a **backlash.**

RODS

Once you've chosen a reel, you must pick a good rod. Lots of times rods and reels are sold as a set, which is great because you know that they are a good match. As a rule, you want a rod with a flexible tip for easy casting. If a rod is too stiff at the tip, it will be hard to cast very far. As you start casting really big lures for big fish, such as northern pike, you'll want a rod with a stiffer tip.

Be careful when choosing a rod for a spinning (open-face) reel. Unlike spincast and baitcasting rods, which have small guides along the rods, spinning rods need to have big guides. Spinning rods also don't have the trigger on the handle like spincast and baitcasting rods.

THE BEST WAY to tie your line to the reel is with an arbor knot.

1 First, loop the line around the spool.

2 Then tie a loose overhand knot.

3 Tie another overhand knot with the free end and snug it up.

4 Pull on your line to make the second knot slip down to the first and tighten against the spool.

Before you can learn how to cast, you first need to put fishing line on your reel. Lots of kids put line on wrong, and they get a big tangle on their first cast. The drawing at left and the photos below show you how to put line on a spinning or spincast reel.

TO PUT LINE ON your spincast or spinning reel, begin by threading the line through the guides of your rod, then tie the line to your spool with the arbor knot (page 42). Next, hold the line tightly with your fingers as you turn the handle on your reel. **1** Have the package of new line lying flat on the floor. If the line gets twisted while you wind, **2** you need to flip the line over on the floor, and start winding again. **3** Don't overfill your reel, because the extra line will become tangled when you cast.

wrong — twisted

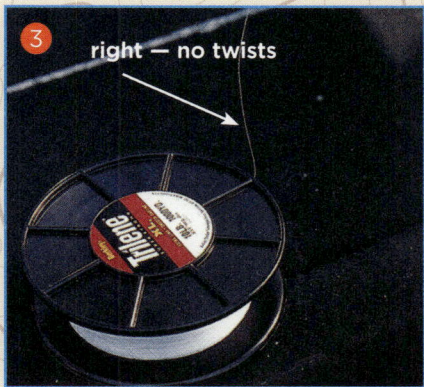

right — no twists

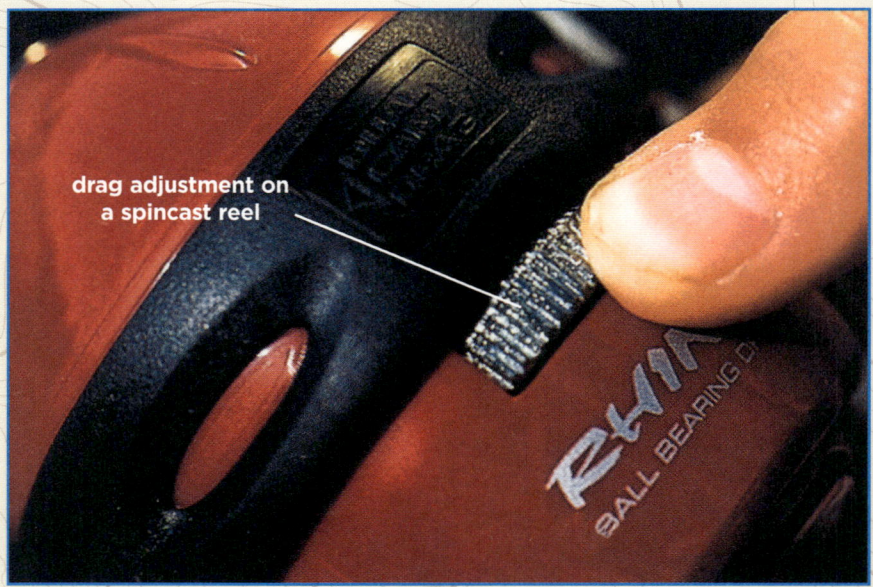

drag adjustment on a spincast reel

An important thing to do, no matter what type of rod and reel you use, is to adjust the reel's **drag.** The drag lets a fish pull fishing line off the reel during the fight before the line breaks. If you use thin line, like 4-pound test, you want your drag set pretty light. How light? The only way to know is to experiment. Grab the line and pull on it about as hard as you think a sunfish can pull. The drag should be set tight enough so line does NOT come off the reel under this light pull. But if you get lucky and hook a nice largemouth bass, it will pull on your line much harder. **Set the drag so some line comes off with a hard pull.**

The people working at tackle shops can also teach you how to set your drag for the size of line you're using. They'd be glad to help.

After you have the drag set on your reel, you're ready to practice casting. You can do this in your yard (if it's big enough) or in a nearby park. Don't cast in the street, because your line will get scratched and weak.

Use the Trilene knot to tie on a **casting dummy** (right). What's a casting dummy? It's a rubber piece with no hooks that weighs about the same as one of your lures.

Check out the photos on the next two pages for tips on how to cast. And always remember: **Look behind you before making a cast.** That way you won't hook anyone, and you won't end up with your line tangled in a bush or tree branch.

HOW TO CAST WITH A PUSH-BUTTON ROD AND REEL

PRESS THE BUTTON with your thumb, and hold it down to keep line from coming off the reel.

BRING THE ROD BACK quickly over your shoulder, stopping at about 10 o'clock.

BRING THE ROD FORWARD with a smooth motion, and release the button with your thumb when the rod is at 12 o'clock. The fishing lure should fly high and far.

HOW TO CAST WITH A SPINNING ROD AND REEL

HOLD THE LINE with your pointer finger, and flip the bail of the reel.

BRING THE ROD BACK quickly over your shoulder and stop at 10 o'clock.

BRING THE ROD FORWARD with a smooth motion, and let go of the line when the rod is at 12 o'clock.

Of all the chapters in this book, this one
will be your favorite. How come?
Because after reading these pages, you'll catch more fish–
a lot more fish!

HOW DO I MAKE A FISH BITE?

Have you ever noticed that sometimes you can use the same
lure or bait as your friend, but for some reason your friend is
getting all the bites, and you can't get a nibble?
What's going on?

Is it the special way your friend is twitching the lure? Or is it
because they spit on their hook before making a cast?
Well, what are you waiting for?
Turn the page and find out!

HOW TO TRICK A FISH

To make a fish bite, you have to trick it. You need to make the fish think that your fake lure is real, or make your live bait look good enough to eat. Most fish are smart, though, so you have to be smart to fool them.

On the next few pages are some of the best fishing setups for tricking all kinds of fish. You'll also see how to work the lures and live bait so they look so good a fish HAS to bite!

BOBBER RIGS

For sunfish and crappies, it's hard to beat a bobber rig. To make one, tie on a small hook or jig using the Trilene knot. Attach a bobber about 2 feet above the hook. Add split-shot to the line about 8 inches above the hook. And don't forget to put bait on the hook!

Make a cast. If you don't get a bite after 10 minutes, move your bobber 1 foot farther away from the hook so that your bait sinks deeper. Still no bites? Move the bobber up another foot and wait 10 more minutes. Keep doing this until you get a bite or get weeds or muck on the hook. If you get stuff on the hook, the bobber needs to be moved closer to the hook.

BOBBER RIG TIPS

HOOK SMALL WORMS several times, leaving the small ends dangling. Break big worms into chunks, and use one piece at a time. Hook a minnow through the back, a leech through the sucker, and a grasshopper through the collar.

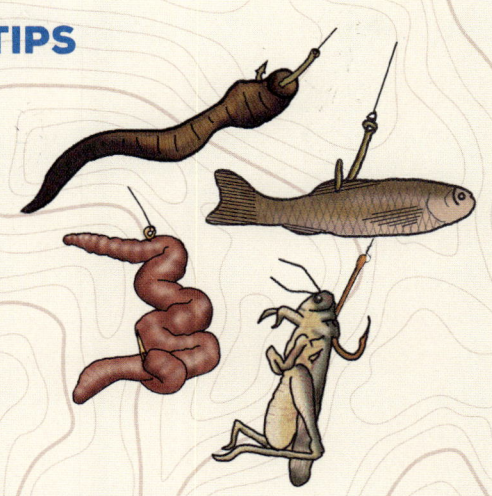

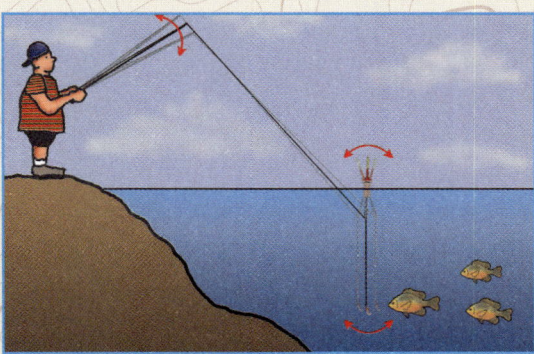

KEEP YOUR LINE from the rod tip to the bobber as tight as possible. This way, when you get a bite, you can get a good pull on the fish.

EVERY 10 SECONDS, move your rod tip to wiggle the bobber. This makes the hook move, which helps fish find the bait.

BOTTOM RIGS

A bottom rig works great for catfish, bullheads, carp, bass, perch, and walleyes. To make a bottom rig, simply tie on a hook, put some live bait on it, and pinch on enough split-shot to sink it to the bottom. If you are fishing a big river or a stream with fast current, you may need a lot of large-sized split-shot to sink your bait to the bottom and keep it in one place.

Make a cast to where you think fish might be hiding or feeding. Keep your line tight to the bottom rig, but don't move it. **Let the fish find your bait.** If you don't get a bite in 15 minutes, wind in your line and cast to a new spot.

BOTTOM RIG TIPS

HOOK A WORM ONCE through an end, a minnow through the lips, and a leech through the sucker. You can also use corn, marshmallows, or chunks of hot dogs for catching catfish, carp, and bullheads.

RATHER THAN HOLDING YOUR ROD AND REEL while waiting for a bite, you can prop it up on a Y-stick. Make sure the Y-stick is tall enough to keep your reel from getting in the dirt or sand. Be sure to sit next to your rod. You don't want a big fish pulling it into the lake before you can grab it!

FISHING A JIG WITHOUT A BOBBER

Jigs can be used without bobbers to catch fish in shallow water, deep water, and everywhere in between. A jig is not the easiest lure to learn to fish with, but once you get good at it, you will catch tons of fish!

Jigs can be used with or without live bait. If you don't use live bait, your jig should have feathers, deer hair, or some type of plastic twister tail to trick the fish into thinking that the jig is alive. The drawings on the next page show the two best ways to fish a jig.

JIG TIPS

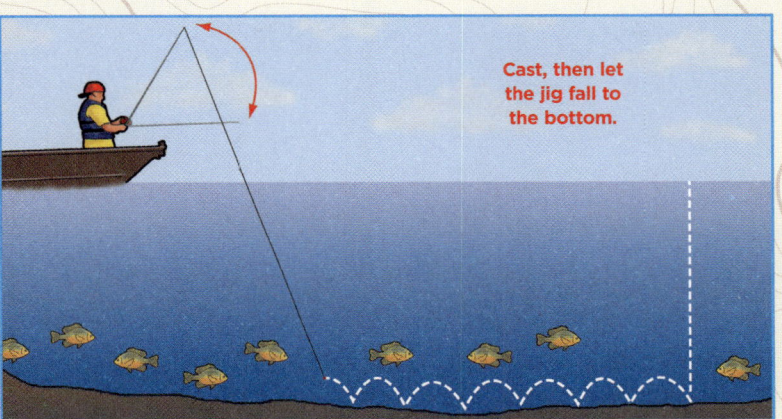

Cast, then let the jig fall to the bottom.

WHEN FISH ARE NEAR THE BOTTOM, it's best to cast out your jig and let it fall all the way to the bottom. Point your rod at the spot your line enters the water, then slowly move your rod tip up to 1 o'clock and stop. This will make the jig hop a few inches across the bottom and then stop. This makes your jig look like a tasty crayfish. Next, slowly wind up the slack line without moving the jig as you return your rod to 3 o'clock. Again, slowly bring your rod to 1 o'clock to move the jig. Repeat these steps until you've brought the jig almost all the way back in. At that point, wind in your line and cast the jig to a new spot.

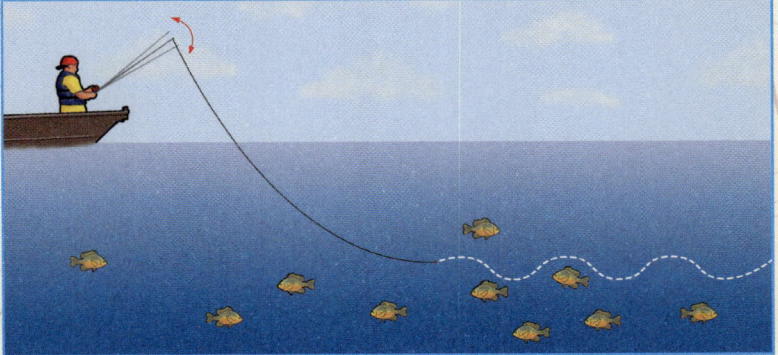

WHEN FISH ARE NOT NEAR THE BOTTOM, try swimming the jig instead of hopping it along the bottom. This makes the jig look like a tasty minnow to the fish. All you do is cast the jig and slowly wind in the line while twitching your rod tip.

FISHING A SPINNER

Spinners come in all shapes and sizes, and they catch all kinds of fish. The lures don't look like anything real, but fish attack them anyway. Many experts think that fish hit spinners because the turning blade sends out a vibration similar to that of a hurt minnow.

Spinners are great because you don't need to mess with live bait, and you can cast and wind them fast. **Spinners are good lures to use when you don't know where the fish are hiding**, because you can cast to a new spot every 10 to 20 seconds.

SPINNER TIPS

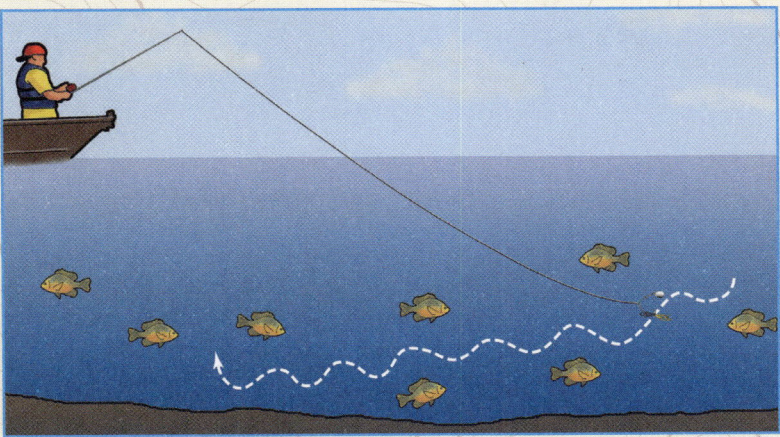

SMALL-SIZED SPINNERS, such as Beetle Spins, work great for sunfish, crappies, perch, and all types of bass. After a long cast, you can wind at a slow speed so the spinner stays 5 to 10 feet below the surface. As you wind, give your rod tip a twitch once every 5 seconds to make the spinner change speeds and direction.

LARGE SPINNERS, such as bass spinnerbaits, won't get easily snagged on weeds. With these lures, all you do is make a long cast, keep your rod tip up, and wind FAST! The spinnerbait should almost come out of the water as you wind. Northern pike and largemouth bass love to eat spinnerbaits that are cranked in fast over shallow weeds.

WHERE TO CAST

There is one simple rule to remember every time you go fishing: **You won't catch a fish if you cast to a spot that has no fish.**

It makes sense, right? So instead of worrying too much about what color lure to use, you would be smarter to worry about exactly where to cast. On most days, the fish aren't picky about lure color. Many times you can switch colors or even change to a totally different kind of lure and keep catching fish. But the moment you cast into a spot that has no fish, you'll catch what? No fish!

It's important to know that each type of fish likes to live in a certain part of a lake or

chapin31/Getty Images

river. For example, if you want to catch sunfish in a lake, you should try casting in a shallow bay with a sand or muck bottom and lots of weeds. But if you want to catch a rock bass, you should try and find a spot on the lake where the bottom is covered with small rocks and sunken logs.

The next few pages will show you where to cast to catch all kinds of fish in lakes, ponds, rivers, and streams. If you take the time to look closely at the maps, you'll have a great chance of catching your favorite fish the next time you make a cast.

WHERE TO CAST IN A LAKE

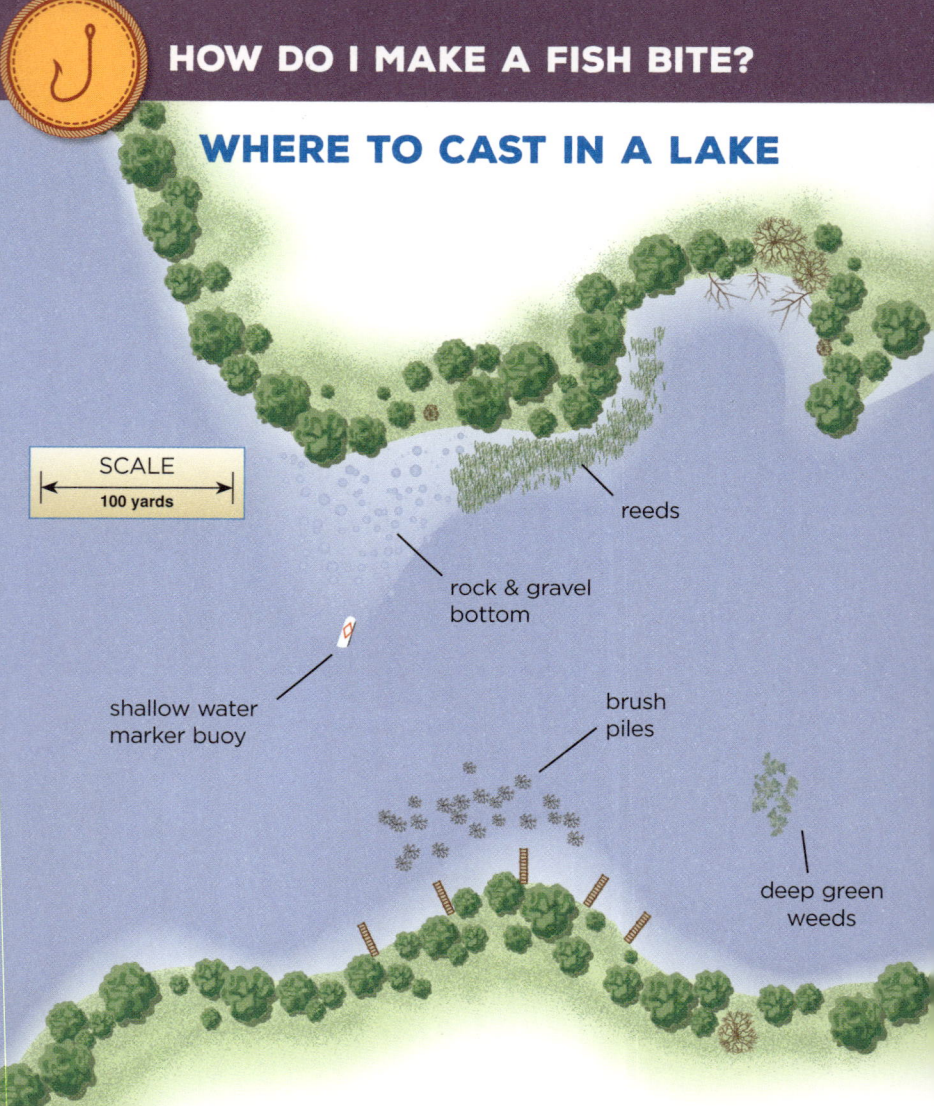

SCALE
100 yards

reeds

rock & gravel
bottom

shallow water
marker buoy

brush
piles

deep green
weeds

In spring, cast to:

- **boat harbors** for crappies
- **lilypad bays** for largemouth bass
- **sand bottoms** for sunfish
- **rock and gravel bottoms** for smallmouth bass and rock bass
- **reeds** for northern pike
- **fallen trees** and brush piles for crappies and largemouth bass

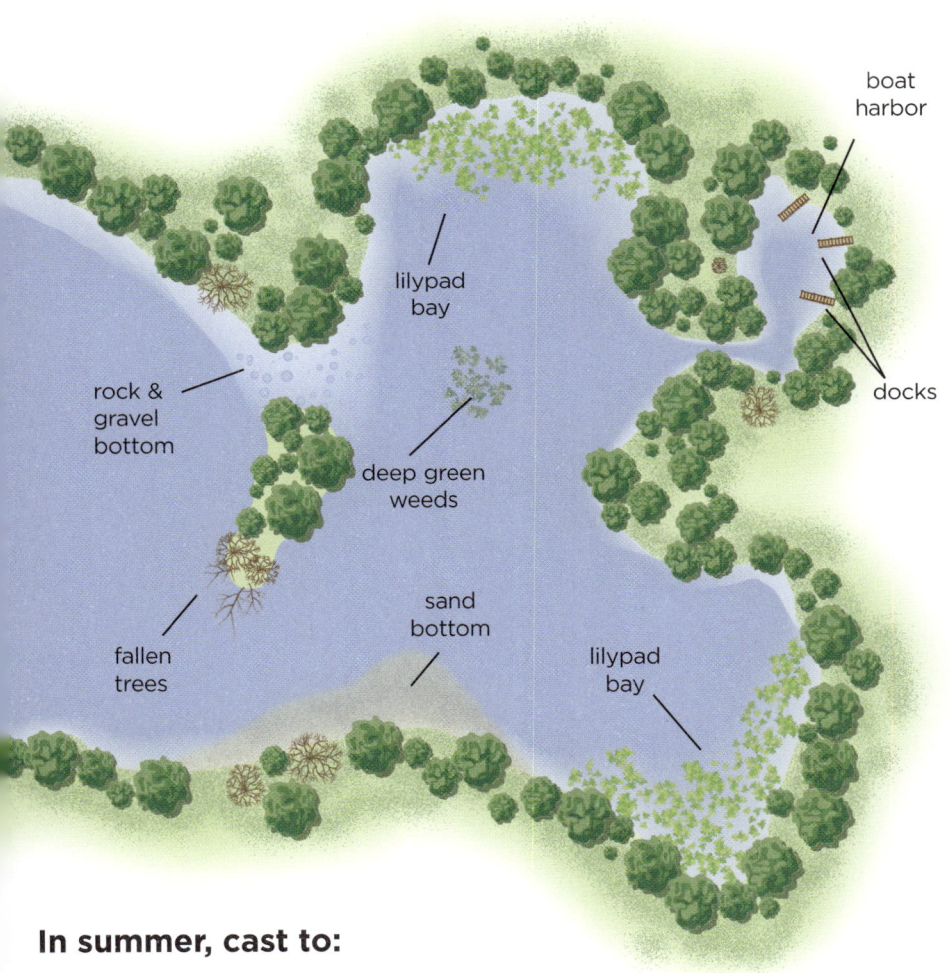

boat harbor

lilypad bay

docks

rock & gravel bottom

deep green weeds

fallen trees

sand bottom

lilypad bay

In summer, cast to:

- **deep green weeds** for sunfish and crappies
- **lilypad bays** for sunfish and largemouth bass
- **boat docks** for largemouth bass
- **rock and gravel bottoms** for smallmouth bass
- **reeds** for northern pike and largemouth bass
- **fallen trees** and **brush piles** for rock bass and largemouth bass

61

WHERE TO CAST IN A POND

deep brush pile

deep hole

deep green weeds

deep brush pile

In spring, cast to:

- **shallow brush** piles and **stumps** for crappies, sunfish, largemouth bass, and catfish
- **docks** for sunfish and largemouth bass
- **shallow weeds** for sunfish and largemouth bass
- **sand bottoms** for sunfish

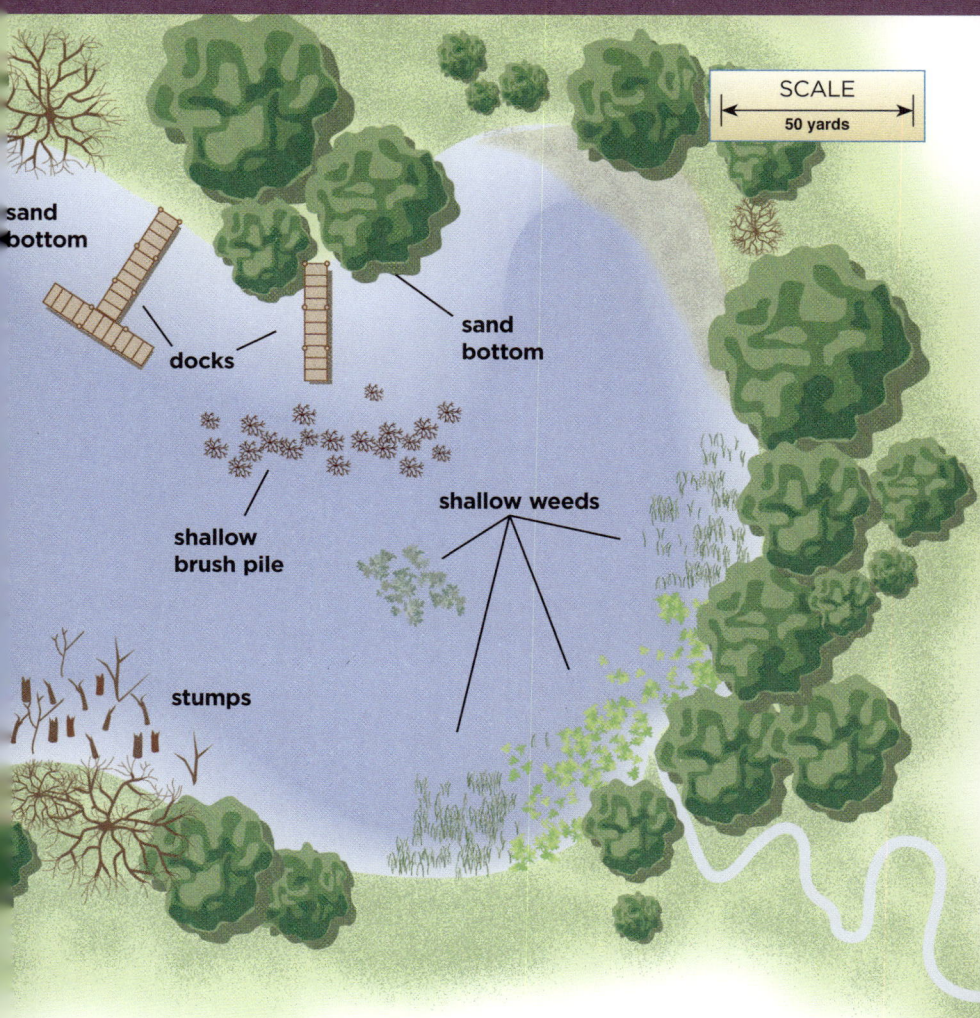

SCALE
50 yards

sand bottom

sand bottom

docks

shallow brush pile

shallow weeds

stumps

In summer, cast to:

- **deep brush piles** for crappies, largemouth bass, and catfish
- **deep green weeds** for crappies and largemouth bass
- **deep holes** for catfish, crappies, and largemouth bass

WHERE TO CAST IN A RIVER

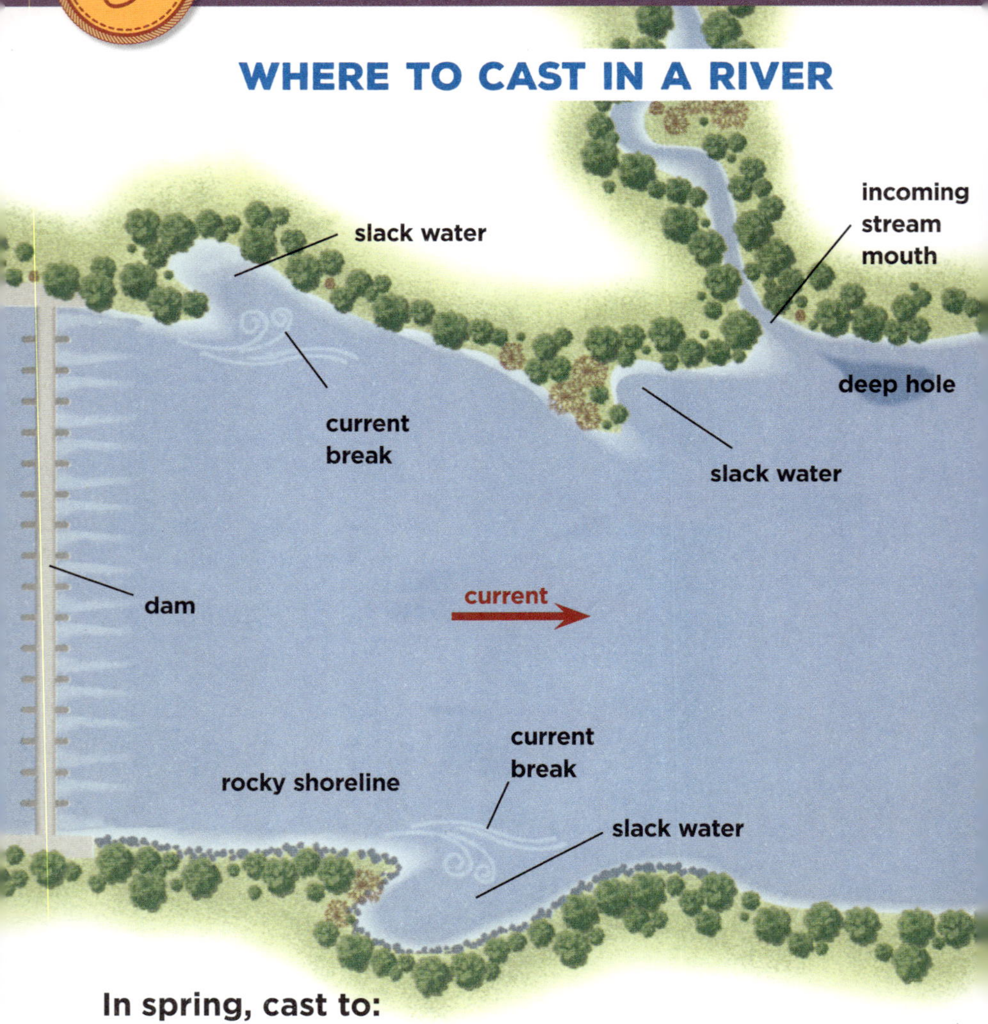

slack water

incoming stream mouth

current break

deep hole

slack water

dam

current

current break

rocky shoreline

slack water

In spring, cast to:

- **backwater stumps** and **brush piles** for carp, crappies, largemouth bass, and northern pike
- **rocky shorelines** for smallmouth bass
- **incoming stream mouths** for carp and northern pike
- **slack water** areas for all river species

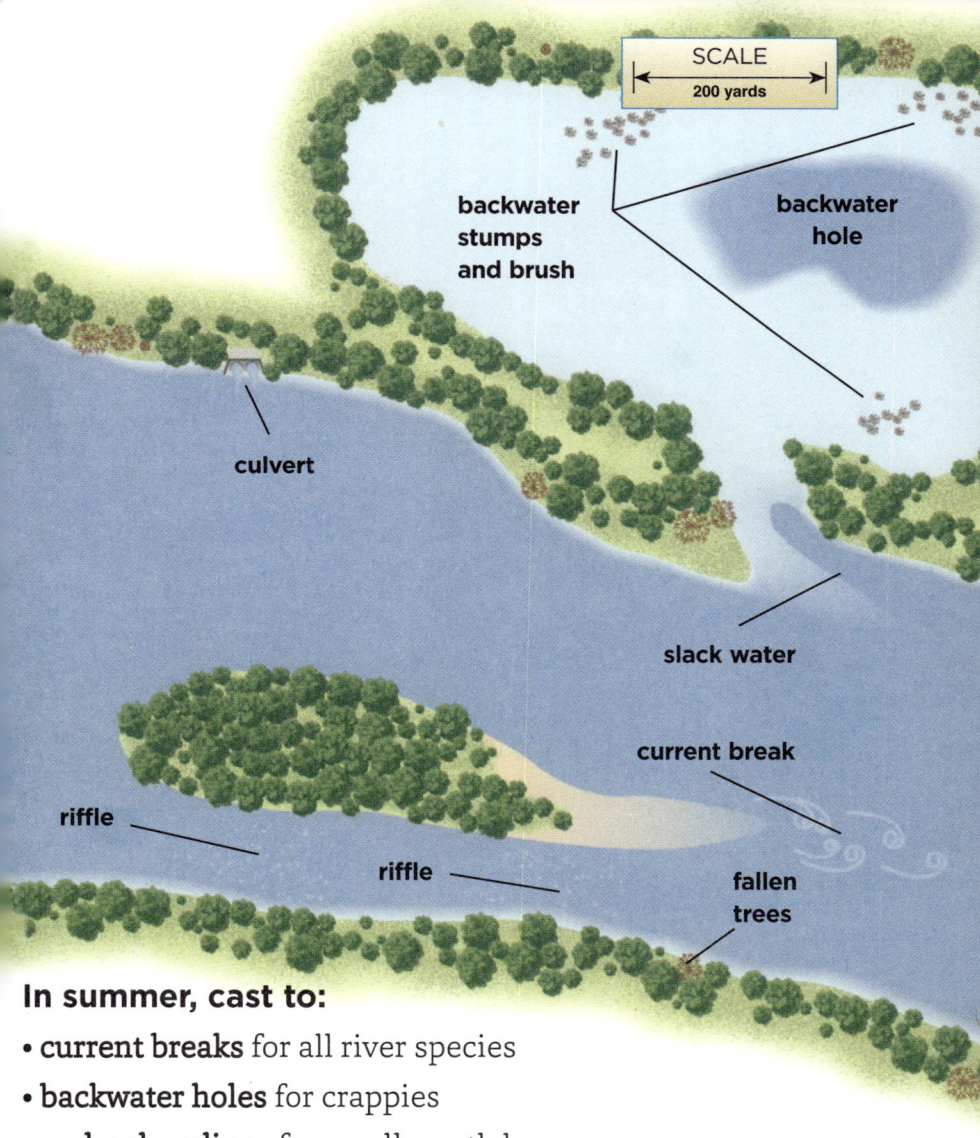

SCALE
200 yards

backwater
stumps
and brush

backwater
hole

culvert

slack water

current break

riffle

riffle

fallen
trees

In summer, cast to:

- **current breaks** for all river species
- **backwater holes** for crappies
- **rocky shorelines** for smallmouth bass
- **riffle areas** for smallmouth bass
- **fallen trees** for catfish
- **deep holes** for catfish
- **culverts** (after a rain) for all river species

WHERE TO CAST IN A STREAM

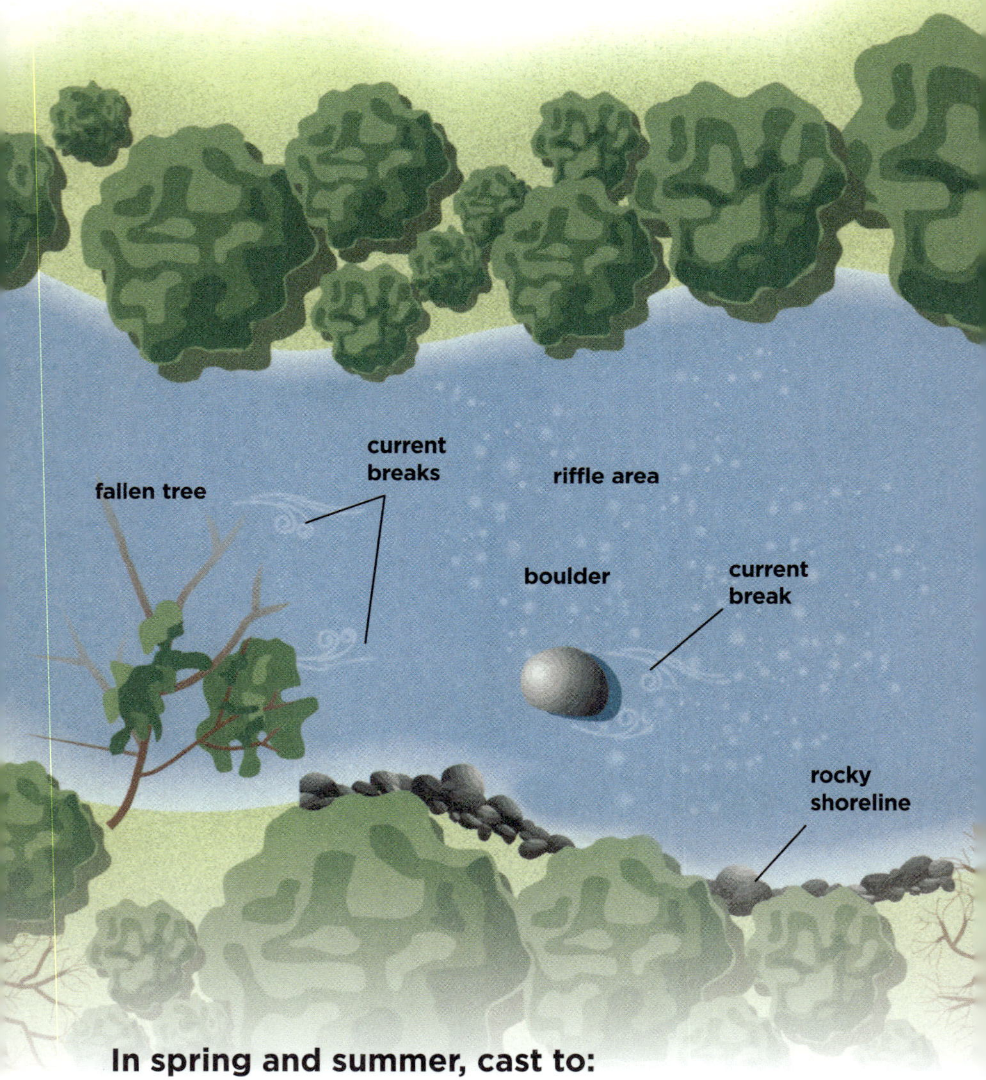

current breaks

fallen tree

riffle area

boulder

current break

rocky shoreline

In spring and summer, cast to:

- **boulders, fallen trees,** and other **current breaks** for all river species
- **riffle areas** for trout and smallmouth bass

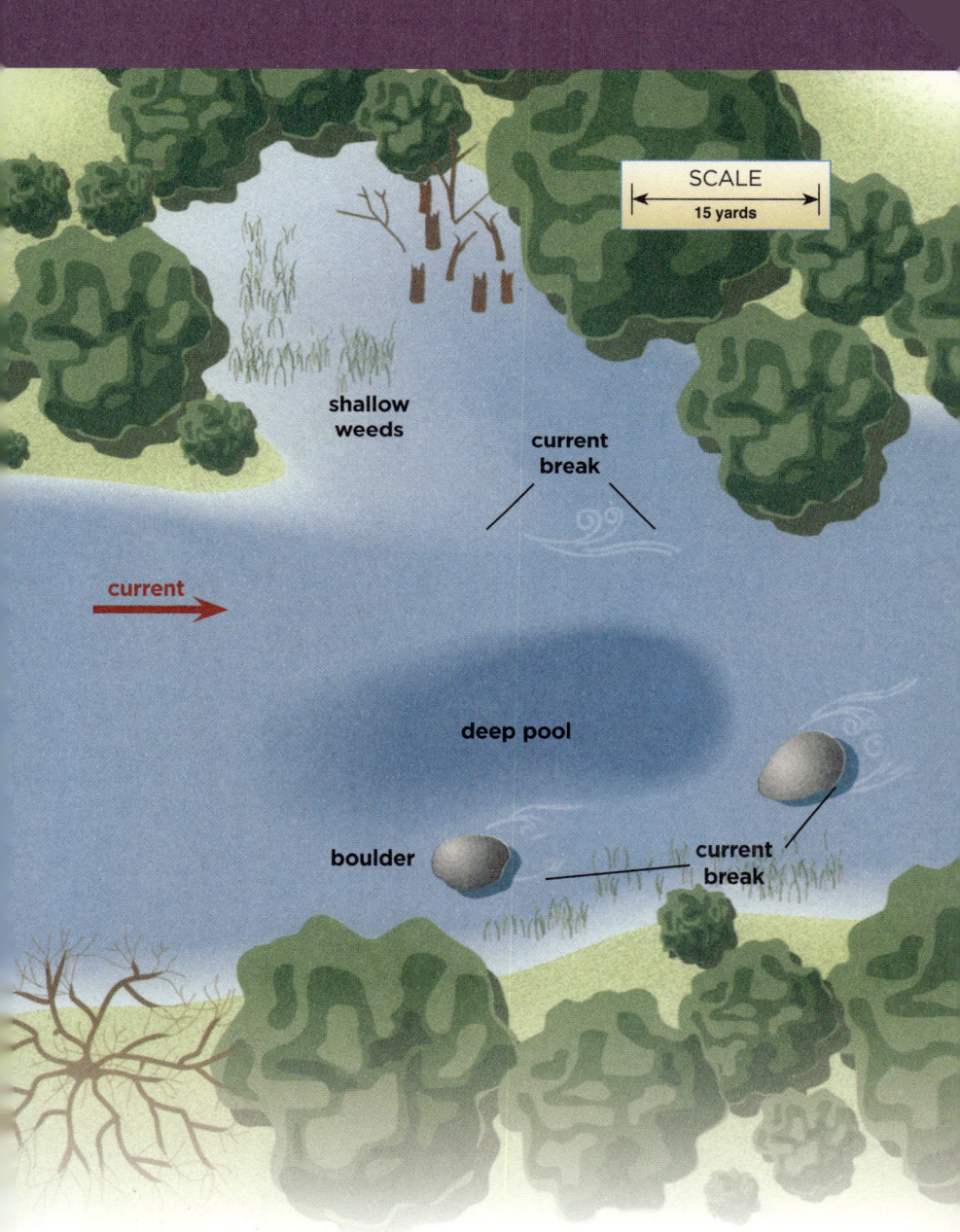

- **shallow weeds** for northern pike
- **rocky shorelines** for trout and smallmouth bass
- **deep pools** for trout and catfish

I THINK I'VE GOT A BITE

If you're like most young anglers, you love to watch the bobber go down. It's exciting because you KNOW a fish has taken your bait. **But the bobber doesn't go all the way down every time a fish bites.** Sometimes the bobber starts moving across the water surface. Should you pull, or should you wait for the bobber to go down? And what if you aren't using a bobber? How do you tell if you have a bite with no bobber?

The pictures on the following pages show you what to watch for when trying to figure out if you have a bite. You will also learn the correct way to pull after you get a bite. This pulling action is called **setting the hook,** and if you do it right, you'll catch almost every fish that bites!

HOW TO TELL IF A FISH IS BITING

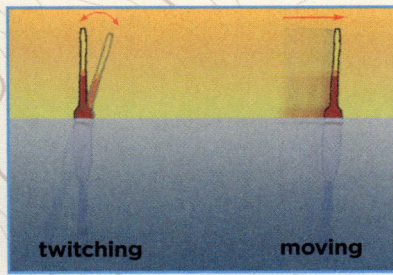

twitching   moving

BOBBER RIG BITES
A biting fish does NOT always pull your bobber all the way under. Sometimes the bobber only twitches a bit, or it starts moving across the water's surface.

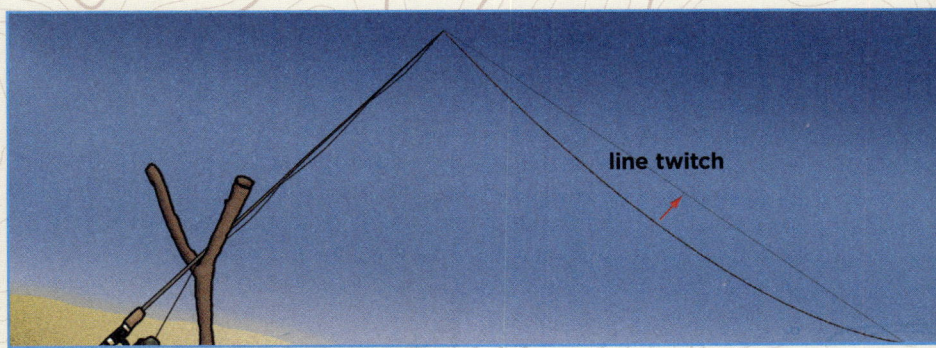

line twitch

BOTTOM RIG BITES Watch the part of your line between the rod tip and the water. When your line jumps or twitches, you're getting a **strike.** When your rod tip starts to twitch, the fish has probably swallowed your bait!

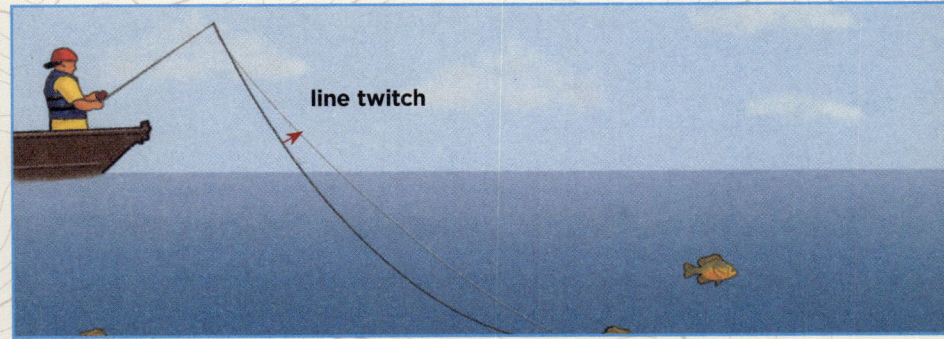

line twitch

JIG BITES The toughest bites to detect are **jig bites.** Sometimes all you'll see is a line twitch. Other times, you'll notice your line moving to the side. But once in a while a fish hits hard enough for you to feel its tug on the rod tip.

WHEN TO SET THE HOOK

If you are using a lure like a spinner or jig without a bobber, you should **set the hook as soon as you get a strike**. The longer you wait, the greater the chance the fish will spit out your lure.

With live bait, you need to wait long enough to be sure the fish has your bait in its mouth, but not too long. If you wait too long, the fish will swallow the hook so deep that it's hard to unhook. So how long is that? As a rule, you should never wait more than five seconds to set the hook. The chart below gives you a good idea of how long to let a fish have your live bait before setting the hook.

TIME-TO-WAIT CHART

TYPE OF LIVE BAIT	TIME TO WAIT BEFORE SETTING HOOK
small piece of worm	1 second
insect	1 second
small minnow for crappies	2 seconds
big minnow for bass	3 seconds
whole nightcrawler for catfish or carp	4 seconds
big minnow for northern pike	5 seconds

HOW TO SET THE HOOK

When it's time to set the hook, quickly move your rod tip to 9 o'clock, and wind up all the slack line. Then quickly set the hook by pulling the rod back to 11 o'clock. Through practice, you'll learn how to set the hook properly!

Steve Debenport/Getty Images

HOW TO FIGHT & LAND A BIG FISH

It's finally happened! You picked the right lure and made the perfect cast. Almost right away you got a bite, and then you set the hook like a pro. Now you have the big fish hooked. What do you do now? Don't panic. Most big fish are lost because anglers get excited and do something hasty. Just take it easy and think a little bit.

The first thing to do is enjoy the fight. If you are too worried about losing the fish, you will forget to have fun. Remember, if you lose the fish, you lose the fish. Big deal. It's not the end of the world. Besides, you were smart enough to hook this one, and you'll hook many more.

The second thing to do after you've hooked a big fish is to **feel how hard the fish can pull.** Don't wind up any line at this point or set the hook again. All you want to do is keep a bend in the rod and let the fish make the first move. You need to tire the fish out before you can land it, and the quickest way to make the fish tired is to let it pull against the fishing rod and the drag of your reel.

What you do next depends on how the fish is acting. If the fish is pulling line off your reel, you should continue to simply hold the rod and let the fish run. Do not try to wind in line if the fish is pulling line off your reel! This puts twists in your line and makes it weak. On most reels, the drag will make a clicking sound if the fish is pulling off line.

After the clicking sound from the drag stops, you should **start to fight back.** But take it slow. Let the rod do the work for you, and the fish will soon get tired. The pictures on the next page show you the best way to fight a big fish.

HOW TO FIGHT A BIG FISH

keep a bend
in the rod

AFTER letting the fish pull a bit, slowly reel up line as you slowly lower your rod tip. But be careful to ALWAYS keep a bend in the rod! This is like tug-of-war, and all you're trying to do is gain a few feet of line on the fish.

NEXT, slowly pull up on the fishing rod like the kid in this photo. Stop pulling when the rod is almost straight up. Continue this tug-of-war battle until the fish gives up.

Once the fish is tired, it's time to land it. Again, don't panic. **The first thing to do is make a plan.**

If you are fishing from shore, the best way to land a fish is to **gently pull it up on shore.** Do not lift it from the water with the rod and line and flip it up on the bank! More than likely your line will break and you'll lose the fish. Instead, just let the fish swim toward shore until it can't swim anymore. Then pull the fish a bit shallower with your rod. If you're going to let the fish go, try and leave most of the fish's body in the water as you take out the hook.

Another good way to land a big fish is to **net it.** But just as when you pull a fish up on shore, if you want to let your big fish free, you should leave both the net and the fish in the water as you unhook the fish.

The last way to land a fish is to **grab it by hand.** You need to be very careful with this method so you don't get a hook in your hand. Make sure you dip your hand in the water before touching a fish so you don't wipe off the fish's protective slime layer.

HOW TO LAND A BIG FISH

BEACH IT. Make sure you leave the fish in a few inches of water as you unhook it. If it's out of the water too long, it might die.

NET IT. Be careful to get the whole fish in the net before you try and lift it out of the water.

GRAB IT. Get your hand wet and grab the fish with a firm grip. Watch out for the hooks!

IS IT A
KEEPER?

Once you land a fish, you have to decide what to do with it.

Do you want to keep it to eat?
Or should the fish be let go?

Before you start fishing, check the laws for the place you are planning to fish and get your fishing license if needed. In many spots, you have to let fish go if they are a certain length. The people who care for the lakes and rivers make these rules to ensure that the fish population remains healthy and the species that live there keep thriving. Fish are an important part of the ecosystems they live in, and it's important to respect that balance—which is why the rules are in place.

And that's why you should **always carry something to measure** the fish you catch. A piece of string with knots tied at certain lengths will work just fine, and is easier to carry than a long ruler.

In this section, you'll learn all about catching and releasing, plus measuring and cleaning the fish you catch.

HOW TO HOLD A FISH

Avoid dorsal fin.

TO HOLD SUNFISH, SMALL CRAPPIES, AND SMALL ROCK BASS, get your hands wet and grab the fish with your palm on the fish's belly. Your fingers should be just below the fish's heads and gills. This way, you avoid the sharp bones of the dorsal fin. If the fish spins on the linewhile you're trying to grab it, hold the lure with one hand to stop the spinning.

It is important to know how to hold a fish the right way. If you do it the wrong way, you may hurt a fish that you want to let go. You also could cut yourself if you put your fingers into the mouth of a fish that has sharp teeth. So you do have to be careful! The pictures in this section will show the best ways to hold all kinds of fish.

There is one rule to always remember: **Wet your hands before touching any fish.** The reason for this is that fish have a slime on their scales that protects them from disease. The slime works a lot like your own skin. If you hold a fish with dry hands, or a dry glove or towel, you'll wipe off this slime. The fish will swim away when you let it go, but it won't take long for disease to attack the fish's body in the spots where you removed the slime. These diseases will kill the fish, so be very careful to always grab fish with wet hands.

CRAPPIES, SUNFISH, BASS, CATFISH, AND BULLHEADS have tiny dull teeth much like rough sandpaper. This is great because you can grab these fish by the top or bottom lip. Just make sure you don't put your fingers or thumb near a hook!

YOU CAN HOLD A CATFISH OR BULLHEAD by the bottom lip or behind the head. When you hold one behind the head, make sure you watch out for the sharp dorsal and **pectoral spines.** These spines can cause a painful wound.

pectoral spines

sharp gill covers

WALLEYES AND PERCH should be held sort of like the way you would hold a small sunfish. Grip walleyes and perch by the belly, but do not get your fingers up around their **sharp gill covers.** Perch have sandpaper teeth, so you can also hold them by the bottom lip. But walleyes have sharp teeth; never grab them by the lip!

NORTHERN PIKE AND MUSKIES have very sharp, long teeth. The best way to hold these fish is by placing your hand over the back of their head. Grip them on the **gill cover**. These fish are super slimy, so you have to hold them a bit tighter than other fish.

FISH LIST

Record the different fish species you catch in your own record book! Be sure to note the species, length, and where and when you caught each one.

Species: Length:
....

Where and when it was caught :
....

Species: Length:
....

Where and when it was caught :
....

Species: Length:
....

Where and when it was caught :
....

CATCH & RELEASE

Answer this question: If you were going fishing for largemouth bass in a small pond, how many bass would you like living in the pond, 50 or 40? Of course, you would want 50. It would be easier to find the bass and get a bite with more of them swimming around.

So let's say you go to a pond that has fifty bass and you catch four bass, which is the most the law in your state will allow you to take home. And let's say your best friend catches three, and your best friend's little brother also catches three. All together, your group has caught ten bass. Not bad!

Now, if all of you keep your fish, how many bass will be left in the pond the next time you go fishing there? Remember math class? Right, 40. (50 − 10 = 40). But if you and your friends let the bass go, the next time you fish the pond, all 50 bass will be waiting for your lures. And there is a good chance that if you catch one of the same bass over again, it will be bigger!

This doesn't mean you have to throw back every fish you catch. For example, sunfish multiply really fast, and if you take some of them home to eat, you won't hurt the total fish population. As a rule, the best fish to keep for eating are sunfish, crappies, perch, walleyes, and catfish. If you are lucky enough to catch a largemouth bass, smallmouth bass, or northern pike, it's a great idea to take a quick photo and let the fish go.

HOW TO RELEASE A FISH

river current

The best way to release a fish like this trout is to gently hold it under the water by the belly or tail. Never drop or throw a fish into the water. If you're releasing a fish in a river, point the fish's head into the current. Let the fish swim away from your hands when it's rested and strong. Trout are very sensitive fish and should always be released carefully.

I'M KEEPING THIS FISH

If you decide to keep some fish to eat, **it's best to try and keep your catch alive or cold.** It's sort of like food that needs to be kept in the refrigerator. For example, say you forgot to put the milk back in the refrigerator before going to school, and it sat on the kitchen table all day. Would you drink it when you got home? No way! The milk would be sour and you might get sick.

Fish are the same way. You can't catch a fish and just throw it on shore, then take it home a few hours later. If you do, chances are good that the meat from the fish will be bad and unsafe to eat. Instead, you should **bring along a stringer or fish basket** and try to keep the fish alive in the water right up until the time you take the fish home. If it's a long trip home, you need to have a cooler with ice to keep the fish cold during your trip.

CLIP-TYPE STRINGERS
are more expensive than rope stringers, but they keep fish alive longer because the fish have more freedom to swim.

WIRE FISH BASKETS are the easiest way to keep fish. All you do is push open the basket's cover and slip in your fish. Remember to have the basket tied off deep enough so the fish stay below the water's surface.

ROPE STRINGERS are the cheapest way to keep fish. Your fish will stay alive for a long time if you keep them under the surface of the water.

HOW TO CLEAN FISH

If your favorite food is pizza, you've never eaten a meal of fresh fish! But **you have to know how to clean your catch** the right way if you are going to have a great meal. After all, no one likes to bite into a fish bone.

The photos on these pages show you the best way to **fillet** (take the flesh off) a fish. **Always have your mom or dad help you when you clean your catch.** A fillet knife is very sharp, so be careful!

HOW TO FILLET A FISH

CUT BEHIND the pectoral fin straight down to the backbone. Angle the cut toward the top of the head.

RUN THE KNIFE along one side of the backbone. The knife should scrape the rib bones without cutting them.

PUSH THE KNIFE through the flesh just behind the rib bones. Cut the piece of flesh free at the tail.

CUT THE FLESH carefully away from the rib bones. To save flesh, the blade should cut right next to the bones.

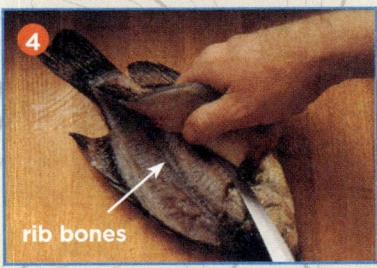

rib bones

REMOVE THE FIRST boneless piece of flesh by cutting through the skin of the stomach area.

TURN THE FISH over. Remove the second piece of flesh using the same filleting technique.

TAKE THE SKIN OFF the flesh, if desired. Hold the tail with your fingertips and cut between the flesh and skin with a sawing motion. Rinse the flesh right away with cold water.

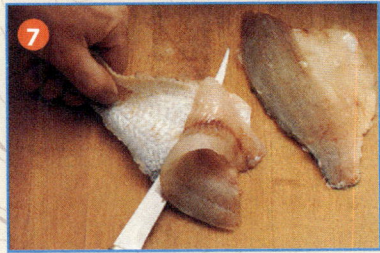

WHAT'S THE RECORD?

Every angler dreams of catching a record fish. No, you wouldn't be as famous as a pro athlete, but the other kids you fish with would be impressed!

First off, you need to understand that there are all kinds of records. For example, there are world records, state records, and line-class records. Huh? Actually, it is pretty easy to understand. Take largemouth bass, for instance. The world record is 22 pounds, 4 ounces. That fish was caught in Montgomery Lake, Georgia, in 1932, by George W. Perry.

A state record is just what it says, a single state's record. If you live in Wisconsin, the state record largemouth bass is 11 pounds, 3 ounces. The state record flathead catfish in Texas is 98 pounds, 8 ounces. Get the idea?

You can usually find out your state's record fish by looking online. These records may also be listed in the handbook of fishing laws for your state, or with your state's game and fish department.

Line-class records are a bit more complicated. These records are kept for a certain pound-test of fishing line. For example, the biggest walleye ever caught on 8-pound-test line was 19 pounds, 13 ounces. The biggest walleye ever caught on 12-pound-test line was 22 pounds, 11 ounces.

You can get a list of world records and line-class records by contacting the International Game Fish Association, 300 Gulf Stream Way, Dania Beach, Florida 33004. This organization will also give you information on how to apply for a record should you catch a huge fish. Good luck!

SPECIES	WHAT IT WEIGHED	WHERE IT WAS CAUGHT
Largemouth Bass	22 pounds, 4 ounces	Georgia
Rock Bass	3 pounds	Ontario, Canada
Smallmouth Bass	10 pounds, 14 ounces	Tennessee
Bluegill	4 pounds, 12 ounces	Alabama
Black Bullhead	7 pounds, 7 ounces	New York
Grass Carp	68 pounds, 12 ounces	North Carolina
Flathead Catfish	123 pounds, 9 ounces	Kansas
Black Crappie	4 pounds, 8 ounces	Virginia
Muskie	67 pounds, 8 ounces	Wisconsin
Yellow Perch	4 pounds, 3 ounces	New Jersey
Northern Pike	55 pounds, 1 ounce	Germany
Chinook Salmon	97 pounds, 4 ounces	Alaska
Brown Trout	40 pounds, 4 ounces	Arkansas

SOME WORLD RECORD FISH

WHAT DOES MY FISH WEIGH? HOW OLD IS IT?

Did you know that by simply measuring a fish's length you can tell what it weighs and how old it is? It's true. Fish scientists have done lots of size and age studies, and now you can use their test results on your fish.

It works like this: Say you catch a big crappie in Minnesota. After unhooking it, you quickly measure it and let it go free. It measured 12 inches from nose to tip of the tail. Now look at the Length/Age chart on the next page for crappies. Find 12 inches in the "North" row (since Minnesota is a northern state), and you can see that your crappie is 8 years old. Now look at the "Length/Weight" part of the same chart. Find 12 inches and you know that your crappie weighed 1 pound.

HKPNC/Getty Images

FISH LENGTH, AGE & WEIGHT CHARTS

Spotted Sunfish

Length in Inches at Various Ages

Age	1	2	3	4	5	6	7	8	9
North	3.8	5.0	5.6	6.3	7.1	7.7	8.1	8.5	8.6
South	4.7	5.7	6.7	7.6	8.1	9.3	—	—	—

Weight in Pounds at Various Lengths

Length	6	7	8	9	10
Weight	.22	.35	.50	.68	1.0

Black Crappie

Length in Inches at Various Ages

Age	1	2	3	4	5	6	7	8	9
North	2.9	5.5	7.4	8.6	9.1	10.4	11.6	12.0	12.6
South	3.1	6.7	9.0	10.6	11.3	11.7	12.6	12.8	13.8

Weight in Pounds at Various Lengths

Length	8	9	10	11	12	13	14
Weight	.30	.51	.68	.84	1.0	1.5	2.4

Yellow Perch

Length in Inches at Various Ages

Age	1	2	3	4	5	6	7	8	9
Length	3.0	4.9	6.7	8.1	9.3	10.0	10.6	11.0	11.2

Weight in Pounds at Various Lengths

Length	7	8	9	10	11	12
Weight	.22	.29	.40	.57	.81	1.2

IS IT A KEEPER?

Rock Bass

Length in Inches at Various Ages								
Age	1	2	3	4	5	7	9	11
North	1.6	2.8	3.9	4.9	5.9	7.7	8.7	9.3
South	2.3	4.6	6.3	7.4	7.8	9.0	—	—

Weight in Pounds at Various Lengths							
Length	6	7	8	9	10	11	12
Weight	.16	.25	.39	.57	.79	.92	1.2

Largemouth Bass

Length in Inches at Various Ages								
Age	1	2	3	4	5	6	8	10
North	4.7	8.5	11.3	13.4	15.3	17.1	19.5	20.8
South	7.5	12.0	15.5	18.2	20.3	22.1	24.9	—

Weight in Pounds at Various Lengths							
Length	12	14	16	18	20	22	24	26
Weight	1.0	1.9	2.7	3.5	5.4	7.2	8.6	9.5

Smallmouth Bass

Length in Inches at Various Ages								
Age	1	2	3	4	5	6	7	8
North	4.2	6.7	8.6	10.9	13.0	14.6	15.8	16.9
South	5.9	10.7	13.5	16.6	18.5	20.4	21.0	21.6

Weight in Pounds at Various Lengths						
Length	12	14	16	18	20	22
Weight	1.0	1.5	2.6	3.9	5.0	6.2

Catfish

Length in Inches at Various Ages

Age	1	2	3	4	5	6	7	8	9
North	5.7	7.1	9.0	10.5	12.3	14.1	15.9	18.4	19.7
South	10.9	13.7	15.7	17.8	19.0	21.6	22.6	23.5	24.3

Weight in Pounds at Various Lengths

Length	12	15	18	21	24	27	30	33	36
Weight	.5	1.3	2.7	3.3	5.8	8.8	11.6	15.3	20.4

Bullhead

Length in Inches at Various Ages

Age	1	2	3	4	5	6	7	8
North	5.3	6.5	8.1	8.9	9.6	11.3	11.8	12.1
South	3.7	6.7	9.0	10.8	12.3	13.8	—	—

Weight in Pounds at Various Lengths

Length	6	8	10	12	14	16	18
Weight	.11	.27	.67	1.1	1.6	2.2	3.0

Northern Pike

Length in Inches at Various Ages

Age	1	3	5	8	11	14	17	20
North	3.2	8.1	12.3	17.8	23.8	29.4	34.1	38.8
South	10.9	23.0	28.3	—	—	—	—	—

Weight in Pounds at Various Lengths

Length	20	25	30	35	40	45
Weight	1.8	3.6	5.8	10.6	16.5	23.9

INDEX

A

Age, Determining, 90
  Charts, 91-93
Arbor Knot, 42, 43

B

Backlash, 41
Bait,
  Choosing, 48-57
  Hooking, 37, 51, 53
  Live, 36-37, 51, 53, 70
  Smell of, 15
  See also: Lures
Baitcasting Reels, 41
  Choosing a rod for, 42
Basket, Fish, 84, 85
Bass, 10-11
  See also:
  Largemouth Bass;
  Rock Bass;
  Smallmouth Bass
Bites, Fish, 68-69
Bobber Rig, 50-51
  Bites, 69
Bobbers, 31, 68-69
Bottom Rig, 52-53
  Bites, 69
Bullheads, 14-15

C

Cane poles, 40
Carp, 12-13
Casting, 46-47, 58-59
  Far, 40, 42
  Lakes, 60-61
  Ponds, 62-63
  Practicing, 45
  Rivers, 64-65
  Streams, 66-67
  Safety during, 25, 45
Casting Dummy, 45
Catch and Release,
  82-83
Catfish, 14-15
Chinook Salmon, 20-21
Cleaning fish, 86-87
Cooler, 84

Crappies, 8-9
  Bobbers, 31
  Depth of,
  determining, 35
  Hooking, 26, 27, 50

D

Depth of Fish, 35
Drag, 44-45, 73

E

Equipment, 22-47
  See also: Bait; Knots,
  Fishing; Lines; Rods;
  Reels
Eyes,
  Crappies, 9
  Rock bass, 10
  Sunfish, 7
  Walleyes, 19

F

Fighting a Big Fish,
  44, 72-73, 74
Fins,
  Crappies, 8
  Perch, 18
  Rainbow Trout, 20
  Sunfish, 6-7
First Aid, 25

G

Gills,
  Sunfish, 7

H

Hats, 25
Holding fish, 25, 75,
  78-81
Hooks, 26-28
  Setting, 70-71
  Size of, 27, 28

I

International Game
  Fish Association, 89

J

Jig, 32, 35
  Bites, 69
  Without a bobber,
  54-55

K

Keeping fish, 76-77,
  84-85
Knots, Fishing, 38-39,
  42

L

Lakes, 60-61
Landing a Big Fish,
  74-75
Largemouth Bass, 11
Laws, 76, 77
Length, Measuring, 76,
  77, 90
  Charts, 91-93
Life Jackets, 24, 25
Lines, 28-29
  Putting on reel, 42, 43
  Size of, 29
  See also: Drag
Lures, 32-35, 70
  Choosing type of, 35,
  48-57
  Size of, 34
  See also: Jig; Spinner

M

Monofilament Line,
  28-29
Mouth,
  Bullheads, 15
  Carp, 13
  Catfish, 14
  Crappies, 9
  Largemouth Bass, 11

Northern Pike, 17
Smallmouth Bass, 11
Sunfish, 7
Muskies, 16-17

N

Netting Fish, 75
Northern Pike, 16-17

P

Perch, 18-19
Ponds, 62-63
Push-button Reels,
  41, 43
  Casting, 46

R

Rainbow trout, 20-21
Records, 88-89
Reels, 41
  Putting line on, 42, 43
  See also: Drag
Releasing Fish, 83
Rivers, 64-65
Rock Bass, 10
  Bobbers, 31
Rods, 42

S

Safety, 24-25
Salmon, 20-21
Set the Hook, 68
  How to, 71
  When to, 70
Shape of Fish,

Crappies, 8
Muskies, 16
Northern Pike, 16
Sunfish, 7
Sides of Fish,
  Bullheads, 15
  Carp, 13
  Catfish, 14
  Chinook Salmon, 21
  Crappies, 8
  Largemouth Bass, 11
  Muskies, 17
  Northern Pike, 17
  Perch, 18
  Rainbow Trout, 20
  Rock Bass, 10
  Smallmouth Bass, 11
  Walleyes, 19
Sinkers, 30
  See also: Split-shot
Size of Fish,
  Bullheads, 14
  Carp, 12
  Catfish, 14
  Chinook Salmon, 21
  Crappies, 8
  Muskies, 17
  Northern Pike, 17
  Perch, 19
  Rainbow Trout, 20
  Sunfish, 6
  Walleyes, 19
Slime, 75, 79, 81
  Sunfish, 6
Smallmouth Bass, 11
Species, 4-21
Spincast Reels, 41, 43
  Casting, 46
  Choosing a rod for,
  42

Spinner, 32, 35,
  56-57
Spinning Reels, 41, 43
  Casting, 47
  Choosing a rod for,
  42
Split-shot, 30
  Bobbers and, 31
  Live bait and, 52
  Spring-lock Bobber,
  31, 68-69
Streams, 66-67
Stringers, 84, 85
Sunblock, 25
Sunfish, 6-7
  Bobbers, 31
  Hooking, 26, 27, 50
Sunglasses, 25, 35

T

Tackle, 22-47
Tails,
  Carp, 12
  Chinook Salmon, 21
  Muskies, 16
  Walleyes, 19
Trilene Knot, 39, 45
Trout, 20-21

W

Wading, 24
Walleyes, 18-19
Weight, Determining,
  90
  Charts, 91-93

READ MORE

Ranger Rick

Check out the Ranger Rick, Ranger Rick Jr.,
and Ranger Rick Cub magazines at
www.RangerRick.com

And get the next guide from Ranger Rick:
Kids' Guide to Camping!

AUTHOR

Dave Maas spent five summers working as an instructor and guide at Camp Fish, an educational fishing camp for kids. Today, he writes about fishing and other passions as managing editor for the popular website OutdoorHub.com. Dave lives with his wife and two sons along the banks of the Crow River in south central Minnesota. No matter the time of year, the entire Maas family is often gone fishin'!

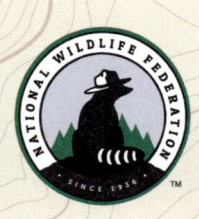

NATIONAL WILDLIFE FEDERATION NATURALIST

David Mizejewski is a naturalist, author and the host of NatGeo WILD's television series **Pet Talk**. As a wildlife expert, he has appeared on many television and radio shows, including **Conan, Good Morning America,** and the **Today Show.** A lifelong naturalist, David spent his youth exploring the woods, fields, and wetlands, observing and learning all about the natural world around us. He lives in Washington, DC.